Cosmic Talk Show II

MORE Channeled Messages from Angels & Spirit (The Arrival is Imminent)

Raymond A. Zachary

Cheryl E. Booth

Contents

Meet the Authors

Raymond A. Zachary

My name is Raymond Zachary, and my background includes working in the electronics, aerospace, and defense industries between 1958 and 2000. I finished my BA in Zoology at the University of Texas in Austin in 1956, and my MA in Mathematics in 1958. My first job was at Boeing in Renton, Washington and it began a career as a computer programmer analyst.

Later I became a team leader at Texas Instruments and completed additional work in Electrical Engineering and other mathematics courses at Southern Methodist University in Dallas. That completed my formal education.

Life progressed and I met the girl that was to become my soulmate. We proceeded through the next 22 years with her practicing her artistic creativity, and me helping out as her mechanical and computer support. Sadly, after a valiant battle with adrenal carcinoma, she passed away. I was left devastated and empty.

I sold our house in California and moved to Texas to be close to my children and grandchildren. Once there, I was referred to the co-author of this book, Cheryl E. Booth. In a psychic medium session with Cheryl, Sharon began giving me amazing information about her experiences in Heaven. I also got messages from my father and other family members there.

Sharon took the lead in introducing me to her activities in the spirit world. We have explored religion, physics, aliens, and the extent, organization, management, and operational concepts of Heaven. I have questions. When I ask a tough one, often an Archangel will take the mic, so to speak, and elaborate at length.

We have discussed aliens and their roles from times in the distant past to the present. A fleet of the Anunnaki are due to arrive sometime in 2022. Their mission is a peaceful one, focusing on assisting humanity in making necessary course corrections.

You are invited to join us as we sally forth into this adventure called LIFE and thank you in advance for coming along. By the way...This is not fiction.

Raymond A. Zachary

Cheryl E. Booth

Greetings and blessings to you! I am so pleased to be involved in this follow-up book to Ray's and my first book together *Cosmic Talk Show* (published in 2021). It contains new messages from the Archangels as well as Ray's family that are different from those in the first volume.

Working as a psychic medium for 35 plus years, I sometimes do channeling, which is what these two books are based upon. The primary Archangels transmitting messages in both volumes are Michael, Raphael, and Gabriel. Other personal messages for Ray come from members of his family in Spirit.

A driving motivator behind this second book is urgency. We have been told that a fleet of friendly Anunnaki are en route to Earth and are due to arrive and be revealed to ALL at some point in 2022. They are on a peaceful mission to help humans make some course corrections as part of their own karmic balancing. (They were not pro-human during their time here in ancient Egypt when several of them served as pharaohs who enslaved the human race).

FYI: I am a long-time fan of the teachings of Esther Hicks and Abraham, and as they are fond of saying, I want to paraphrase them and say to you: We are presenting this information for those who are seeking it.

Just a little background on me...I was raised in the Midwest, brought up in full-fledged evangelical, speaking in tongues, Pentecostal church. You may well be able to imagine that my being a psychic child did not exactly mesh well with my mother's deep subscription to our religion! In fact, it was a primary source of our clashing and misunderstanding one another throughout my youth. She passed away when I was not quite 16 years of age, but for many years now, the two of us have had a lovely, healed, and continually expanding connection, for which I am eternally grateful.

You can read more about my family and background in my book *Johnny Angel Is My Brother: A Psychic Medium's Journey.* It is available on Amazon. I am currently in the process of updating it to reflect events that have occurred since its original printing in 2006. If you'd like to read more about my work as a medium, please visit my website www.cherylebooth.com

There you'll read testimonials about my work, the various services I offer, and more.

In addition to readings, I provide hypnotherapy, life coaching, grief counseling, psychic mentoring, and conduct past life regressions.

If you'd like to read more about my writing, please visit www.shiningwrite.wordpress.com It contains information on the five books I've written or contributed to in the past, as well as the fact that I currently also write screenplays and stage plays.

Ray and I hope that you'll find upliftment from the messages in this book as well as the first one. A few of those messages may cause you to pause, scratch your head and ponder a bit. We're not interested in changing or challenging your belief systems, simply in presenting information that we feel deserves a voice. Enjoy, and bless you!

Cheryl E. Booth

www.cherylebooth.com

www.shiningwrite.wordpress.com

https://www.amazon.com/author/cherylebooth

Introduction

This book serves to do three things. First, you will find conversations not included in the messages of the first *Cosmic Talk Show*, released late in 2020. Cheryl and I feel that these newer messages are important enough to merit this second book of conversations with the Archangels.

Secondly, there are significant additional questions of importance that need exploring to enhance what has been revealed previously.

Finally, mankind is about to encounter aliens in a way that is up close and personal (predicted for some time in 2022). In this book, we have addressed several subjects that should help smooth the way to mankind's enlightenment and adjustment to the new reality.

This book endeavors to prepare humanity for a great awakening that is expected to alter the paradigm of thinking about almost everything that affects the whole of Earth's population. We may not all be ready for what's coming, but we owe it to ourselves to give it our best effort to prepare.

Introduction

There were eight parts to the first book; this book starts with Part 9 and continues through Part 17.

PLEASE NOTE: There are FREE Bonus Audios from Cheryl that you may claim at the end of the book. They are designed to help you stay balanced and centered in these uncertain times, and to help you strengthen your own ability to communicate with those in Spirit, should you so desire. So be sure to check them out!

Part 9: Upgrading Mankind

On Upgrading Mankind with a Soul

R: I believe I read that the Anunnaki made the decision to upgrade their earlier version of mankind to have a soul. This would imply that they knew the nature of a soul and the genetic requirements of a being to pair with a soul. They would also have to have acknowledged their own nature as a living soul equipped with free will.

One question that comes to mind is whether the availability and deployment of souls is a willful act of the Creator or His agents, or the result of a somewhat automatic process built into the nature of the resource of souls at their inception. The former would imply that the Creator must approve the deployment on a case-by-case basis, whereas the latter implies that anyone intelligent enough to create a viable being would enjoy the right to equip that being with a soul. What do you say about all this?

C: Gabriel is the one stepping forward first to respond. He says that beings without a soul are the equivalent of what man is playing with now with Artificial Intelligence. While it might be satisfactory on some levels to see the results of your labor, without the ability to have a personality and a soul living within such a being, it is kind of a hollow achievement.

So, it does feel that the Anunnaki realized that just having automatons or robotic beings to be a slave race was prone to breaking down after a certain amount of wear would take place. And without cognizance within the beings to understand how to rest, repair and heal, they were not getting the ultimate desired results. They realized that there was a risk factor involved in imbuing those beings with souls because there might be more readily arising rebellions within the ranks there. Ultimately, they decided that the trade-off was worth it.

It feels that the Creator approved or allowed them to kind of pull from what they've referred to before as sort of this "primordial soup of souls" to infuse into beings knowing that then they would not be satisfied with being a slave race any longer. So that led up to the Age of Enlightenment and the Renaissance.

It feels that there definitely were souls present long before that, but what they're showing me is that even back to the time of Neanderthals and troglodytes, there were not fully realized souls at that stage of man's evolution.

R: I think they anticipated my second question because this issue had to be debated by the Anunnaki. They must have agreed to disagree at some point on how mankind, intended to be a workforce, should be managed with a soul that allows free will to be exercised. So, in other words, mankind could not be both an enslaved workforce and exercise free will at the same time.

This issue came up slightly differently in the history of slavery in the United States, particularly, whether to allow slaves to learn to read and write. It's possible that the first generation of man did not have a soul and was a managed workforce, but it became desirable to give men features of free will souls to improve productivity. Perhaps that was the Anunnaki dilemma. Is that what you're trying to tell me?

C: Yes, they say that that's exactly in the range of what they were trying to explain.

Part 10: Update on Being in Heaven

Sensing Mortal Feelings

R: I have a question for Sharon. It's kind of a technical question.

When you join me when I take Baxter for a walk, sometimes you're there with me and I appreciate that. I am curious about when you're walking with me, and I feel either cold or hot due to the weather. Do you feel or sense what I feel as a part of telepathy or is telepathy limited to the thinking process alone?

C: She says, "No, but I can read your body's rays or aura." She says it's almost like she can see a spectrum of color around you that indicates what sort of touch-sensitive response your body is having to the temperature. So, she doesn't necessarily feel it with you, but she can tell when you are experiencing it.

And she says, "Sometimes I will just put a thought in your head, like, 'Zip that coat up the rest of the way,' or things you maybe didn't even think about until you realize you're a little cold or whatever. She's doing her best to just keep you healthy, adjusted and comfortable

4

when you're walking. But she says she can get a sense only because she's requested it of her guides... to be able to kind of feel the Earth beneath her feet as she walks beside you.

She said she can also float beside you, in back or in front of you too, if she would choose to do that. That's a little easier, but she says it takes more focus and concentration on her part; more sense memory really than feeling it so much in the moment along with you, but she wants to do that. She wants to keep pace with you and feel as much as she can of what you're feeling.

R: That's absolutely great. I'm sorry for the burden, but I appreciate the effort.

C:Oh, she says it's no burden. She says, "I miss walking on the Earth and that solid 3D feeling beneath your feet. So, it's my choice." She does nothing that you need to apologize for.

Heavenly Training

R: Is she taking any new courses?

C: That's really interesting. She's showing me that they don't really have waiting lists over here per se, like they do to enroll for classes on the Earth plane. But sometimes you must go through a certain number of different kinds of training to prepare for an end goal.

There's a class that's like weaving that she's playing with. Now she says, "But it's not weaving thread or tangible material. It's weaving light and color into a tapestry, that's sort of preparation for being able to do weaving on the Earth plane... using clouds, colors and other elements that will catch your attention, as well as specific other people that are connected to her, when you and other loved ones look up in the sky.

Or if they look at a grove of trees ahead of them and see some unusual rays of light and color unlike anything they've seen before, she will have had a hand in that. So, she says, she's really been enjoying that, even though it feels like weaving thread. When she was here, weaving was not something she was exceptionally interested in, but she says this is a whole new level, a whole different ball game.

R: Sounds like she's saying that she trains with light in a sort of a laboratory environment to manipulate things in the 3D universe.

C: I feel her nodding. Yes. That's pretty close to nailing it on the head, she says. It just requires a few more intermediary steps to work your way up to the end result. She adds that it's very engaging, fun and, more beautiful in many ways than some of the artwork that she did when she was here. But she says it's temporary. She says it doesn't really make her sad, but you work so hard to concentrate, focus and make it happen, and then it doesn't last. It's not something that will continue to hang around like art on Earth. Rather, it's more to just help you and others that are spiritually sensitive that she loves here to have something beautiful to notice, even if it's just for a minute or two.

R: I wonder if there were a prototype of a special cloud formation or something like that, would she nudge me or ask one of her support angels to nudge me to see by projecting a thought like, "Pay attention. Look up in the sky."

C: Yes, she says. Otherwise, that would be a big waste, wouldn't it? For example, if you're looking off to the side and then something makes you feel, "Look up, or look ahead." You'll get the message one way or the other. She says when you are on your walks with Baxter too, that he sometimes will get excited and start barking, and there's nothing that you can see. But if you look in the direction where he is looking, then a lot of times you'll be able to understand what's going on.

She just loves that you and he are such good buddies. She says and she's so grateful that you have each other, because he knows you

6

seldom feel out of sorts or are physically dealing with something that you're not really good at coping with. But when you are having a low energy day, Baxter senses it and knows it. Then he sticks really close to your side, even more than usual on those particular times. He's an intuitive little guy.

R: That is interesting and rewarding, actually.

Heavenly Excursions

R: I would like to ask her if she's engaging with any of the other family members in Heaven on taking trips to the Arctic Circle or anything like that.

C: She says, yes, especially during the times of the Aurora Borealis, when that's prominent in those regions. That's when they tend to kind of plan an outing together. Again, it's light and color. And she says, "I feel that the Earth plane is finally starting to be more appreciative and notice those elements more now than ever before. That's part of what they feel. This whole COVID mess is helping humans to become more aware of our environment and of the natural wonder that we have in the past tended to ignore. Just taken for granted."

So, during those seasonal events, phenomenal things like that, she says that's when they tend to say, "Okay, instead of going on a cruise, let's go on a journey and just kind of be part of this event in the sky, part of the light, to experience it.

R: That's great.

On Learning to Relax in Heaven

R: I would like to talk to my dad. The last time we talked, when I asked him what he was doing, he said he was perfecting the fine art of relaxation, which was like a new course of existence. I wonder how that's going and if he's got any other projects now.

C: Well, he says that that has been a real eye-opener as far as how important it is to stay in balance; to relax and understand how that feels. Not that they stress out or get exhausted over there, but he says, "We are sort of like a candle wick burning very low and close to the surface. Our energy can ebb, but we don't really feel exhausted like the human body when it's just been put through the mill." He says it continues to be interesting and revealing for him.

Regarding other projects, he says he's very interested in the fact that here on the Earth plane there are more groups and organizations that are turning their attention to the oceans and working on harvesting new food sources.

R: Just like taking care of the land.

Is There Challenge in Heaven?

R: I'm a person that seems to need a project or two to keep my energy focused. Therefore, when I think of Heaven, I think there ought to be ways to channel spiritual energy. There should be no shortage of these ways, but because there is no time in Heaven, it may be true that one can simply enjoy eternal peace without challenge. I personally cannot reasonably contemplate that, so I think I would be searching for challenge.

Your role as Archangels seems to be full of perpetual challenge. Am I correct that you guys never approach boredom?

C: Michael is saying that that is so. "We have so much on our plates all of the time, but that is basically why we were created, to be continuously engaged and helpful while we also are learning at the same time." But he says, yes, just as there is truly no need for sleep in the spirit world because of the lack of fatigue in a human body for example, there's also no room for boredom.

Babies in Heaven

R: Sharon, when little babies show up in Heaven, have they been born before? In other words, are there babies that were aborted? Or do you only get babies that were born?

C: She says that it varies. The souls that volunteered or wanted to be born knew that when they did on the other side, there was a possibility that physical circumstances or the decision of one, or both parents, might change that. So, even if they were aborted or miscarried, then the soul still survives and comes back into Heaven.

She's showing me they appear somewhat in a state of a toddler in their spirit body. They're not necessarily needing to be coddled and carried and taken care of, to the extent that babies on the world on the Earth plane are. But they're still quite young, even though their soul is older. She adds, "It's just sometimes the shock of them finding themselves back in that dimension. They need some guidance on whether it will be okay with what happened that prevented their mission's completion. This helps them decide if they want to try again right away. Or if they would rather stay over there and kind of grow up in the spirit world instead.

On Heavenly Appearance

R: Sharon, you've said that most people in spirit choose to appear in their 30s, but that begs the question: which version are you? The latest one or a reincarnated one?

C: She says, typically, it's the last Earthly experience that that someone has had, mainly for the ease of recognizability... "When we do appear in loved ones' dreams that are still there on the Earth plane, or in a vision to them." She knows, Ray, that you have had occasion since she's been in spirit at least a couple of times she's aware of, that you thought you saw her walking down the street from you, or maybe in a store or across a room. These are two episodes she's citing, and that it's possible to see your loved ones, but it's typically from a distance when they're making an Earthly appearance. She feels like you've had that happen a couple of times. Is that accurate?

R: Well, I occasionally see someone that catches my attention because it looks like her. But I've never known that. I hadn't even thought about it being her. I thought about it because my suspicion is that in the great scheme of things, there are not an infinite number of faces. There are probably thousands, and they're replicated, because of the gene code, that part of the gene code gets replicated in civilization. So, I'm not surprised when I see look-alikes, but it catches my attention nonetheless, of course.

Reincarnation Gender

R: I was wondering, have all her reincarnations been female, and have all of mine been male?

C: She says, "Well, you wouldn't learn much if that was the case now, would you?"

R: That's the reason I bring up the question, because you have empathy for the other guys and gals. Where does that empathy come from, right?

C: Yes, she's showing me one of her past lives that she's learned about. She says that she wasn't really in touch with or aware of it when she was here. It was as a troubadour, a wandering minstrel, and she was male.

R: She also said I was one of those too, right?

C: I'll ask her. "Ray asks, Sharon did the two of us know each other in that lifetime then?" She said absolutely. She said you teamed up and you were both male in that lifetime, but it feels like you were friends, not blood relatives. You just decided it was safer to travel around through some potentially rough unknown country together and kind of have each other's back rather than to do it, you know, solo.

She's showing me this might have been in Russia or over in that part of the world because I'm seeing heavy fur coats that you would wear if you had to sleep in a barn, or when you were traveling if you had to find a shelter, then you would cover up with some kind of fur clothing.

Thinking About Past Lives

R: Sharon, do you have conscious memories of past lives? In other words, do you have to do anything special to bring a past life memory into focus?

C: She says, "Mainly it's akin to hypnotherapy and regression that people do on the Earth plane. It's about just relaxing and stilling the mind; going to a different plane of consciousness where you're not fully engaged with your most recent lifetime, or with loved ones that are still on the Earth plane. You just put yourself in a kind of a bubble where you can allow these memories to come to the forefront and just watch them." She says she doesn't really re-experience them. It's more like watching a movie.

R: That's interesting, because that correlates with something one of the Archangels said to me in a past conversation when I asked if all the memories of past lives of an individual were stored in the Hall of Akashic Records for retrieval, in case of needing a reference. And it could be that when she's talking about a kind of escape mode, she's pairing up with the Hall of Akashic Records.

C: She says you're on the right track there. "It is just as when physical beings are wanting to do a regression and tune into these memories. They can't do so effectively if they are distracted by current daily activities, so they must rely on the guidance of a regression therapist to go into this altered state. But over here, we don't really need somebody to conduct it unless that's a particular preference or desire on our part over here. There are others that can do this with us, but you can just choose to create this sort of bubble effect where you are isolated for a time from all distractions and allow those memories to come to the forefront."

Is Reincarnation Earthbound?

R: Sharon, you have suggested in earlier conversations that when I get there, we're going to do some planning and decide what to do with the rest of our existence, and that includes the possibility of reincarnation. I just wondered because I have concerns about reincarnation, with no real reason except uncertainty. I'm wondering if you've explored this whole concept and thought about it. And are we going to have a discussion?

C: Well, she says, "Of course, don't be silly. I won't make a decision like that without you and without your input. But there's no reason to be frightened about it because it is something that we will jointly decide. We would plan it so that we would come to the Earth, or possibly to a different planet or galaxy together into a different world that is more pristine than the current Earth plane that hasn't been discovered, developed, or populated yet, or whatever the case may be. But there's really nothing to be concerned about, honey."

R: Actually, what you have suggested sounds rather exciting to consider.

Part 11: The State of Things

This part addresses where we are in multiple areas of concern.

What Happened With the Greys, et al

R: Previously I brought up the report that Ambar Anati (AKA Victoria) had visited the secret underground AF base at Dulce, New Mexico and discovered serious abuses of the humans by the aliens housed in that facility. That event was confirmed by you. There was no timeline at that time, but recently I have learned that a geologist named Phil Schneider, an AF contractor, was leading a team to explore and plan the expansion of that facility deep underground.

He made a presentation in Idaho on May 8, 1995, detailing an unexpected encounter with several alien Greys and alien Reptilians in 1979 resulting in a firefight where 67 FBI and Black Beret personnel were killed. Schneider was one of three survivors. Eight months later he was reported as a suicide when he was found in his apartment with rubber tubing wrapped around his throat. This story

is covered in detail at multiple Google websites under the query
<Phil Schneider>

If any of this previous narrative is true, it appears that Schneider was a victim of retaliation for speaking out, and Ambar Anati's visit was subsequent to 1995 and the destruction of the deep underground Dulce facility would have occurred at the time of her visit.

Furthermore, the addition of the presence of Reptilians to the mix brings to mind whether those Reptilians were banned from the planet like the Greys (for their abuse of humans) or were they banned to other underground dwellings, as some have reported? I am not sure, but it is possible that some Greys were limited to underwater cities where they would be shielded from sunlight. Is this narrative correct, so far?

C: Yes, I'm getting this from Michael. He's saying affirmative on that, and that Schneider's death was staged. It was not a suicide, and it was symbolic that they silenced his voice by wrapping that tubing around his throat.

Collusion

R: Okay, according to Phil Schneider, multiple treaties were signed with aliens by the government. The years 1944, 1954, 1962, and 1979 were the dates given for these treaties, with the year 1956 being reported as the date of the treaty with the Greys. Given that the Greys have been banished by the Creator, who remains? Schneider reported that there were seven benevolent alien species living on Earth, and four non-benevolent or evil. What do they say?

C: They said there's a reason the government wanted to hush him up because this was not knowledge that they felt the general public could wrap its head around or understand. But essentially the research that you have done is accurate.

Problems with Government

R: It is clear the Earth is fraught with problems that threaten the well-being and lives of people everywhere. But the nature of most of the problems is that governments spend most of their energy in preserving power, and little in unleashing the power that freedom brings, leaving most humans in a state of slavery.

Is there any part of the agenda of the Annunaki or other aliens that addresses this problem as an essential part of the pacification of mankind? Is there no recognition that restricting government to keeping humans free (as God created them) to learn and grow in exercising free will is an essential ingredient to peace and well-being?

C: There is a component of that, that they intend to bring to light, and a large part of this is again, that course correction or rectification that they themselves were guilty of in enslaving mankind and creating a slave race to serve their own purposes back in ancient Egyptian times, in particular.

And so, it feels that they are on a mission to help teach equality and to do so in demonstrable ways; to encourage perhaps the cultivation of more schools, universities, and think tanks in more remote locations in the world, to prove on an intellectual plane that when given opportunity, human beings are more equal than we tend to give each other credit for. No one deserves to be enslaved in any way, so it does feel like this is part of the Anunnaki agenda

A part of their karmic retribution, too, is to raise awareness of "We are all one."

Politics

R: In the process of self-governance, democratic populations generally believe how they vote affects the well-being of their society. However, given the influence of aliens on the elected officials, the question arises whether the alien influence has a positive or negative effect, and whether the effect is significant. Furthermore, it is not clear if beings such as yourselves counter or reinforce alien influences or are otherwise not in the game. Comments?

C: This is gonna upset a lot of people's apple carts. The illusion of the democratic process needs to be in place for the time being to avoid anarchy. However, those who sit in the places of authority for the larger world powers are put in place because factions such as the World Banks and other associates of the Illuminati want them to be there.

R: This is not a surprise.

C: No, not to you. But for many people, it will rock their world. So, the alien intervention with them has always been with the most powerful rulers. They have always been, not necessarily open at first, but from the aliens' point of view, they have been in their sights as far as those to visit and attempt to influence. But they say they have skipped some of the lesser rulers that were not respected as much or did not have as much influence over the people.

That's why you hear about Truman and Eisenhower having visits from aliens, but as for others, it's much more on the hush-hush whether they did it or not. Not every single president, certainly not every single sheik, pharaoh, or ruler of other places has had an alien visitation.

R: The Annunaki implemented Kingship as a form of government, and the outcome appears to have depended on the morality and competence of the Annunaki person overseeing the appointed king. In recent history, democracy was instituted as a test of mankind's ability at self-government. That has been predicted to last at most about 200 years due to the short sightedness of the electorate. So far, the data would tend to verify that prediction although the conclusion has yet to be fully tested in the USA. What do you say?

C: Initially the democratic process of voting and so forth was pure, the intention of it was pure but the efficacy of it started being messed with. Right from the beginning, with ballot boxes being stuffed and arranging to get corrupt people in power that they felt could do more for them. So, they're asking, "Has the Electoral College ever really worked on some levels? We must say no, and certainly not for about the last 30 or 40 years in this country. In particular, it has been far from a true test of how people are put into the White House." They said most noticeably the last 30 or 40 years, but really beginning in a large way from the turn of the 20th century.

R: By my reading, it's about 100 years.

Philosophy and Politics

R: There seem to be two polarized thought forms on Earth: One is that we are individuals with a God-given right to be free of coercion to become the best that we can be. This thinking leads to so-called "free societies" with an institutionalized respect for human individualism and personal responsibility.

The other thought form is that our needs, however subjective, are the responsibility of the collection of all of us – we must conform to the common good as defined by some authority, that is usually government. This latter thought form seems to be at the root of all national monetary failures and wars. Do you guys see it differently?

C: They're saying that's a pretty good summation that you've presented there, Ray, and that while war is very heinous and distasteful to the Creator's energy, it has in some ways always been a necessary evil; to allow the beings not just on the Earth, but in other planetary regions as well, to have a choice – to have a clear-cut decision that they can make about aligning with the dark or with the light, as far as energy forces and intentions go.

Earth has been so beleaguered by war for so many centuries – pretty much ever since human population was brought forth...Michael is saying he doesn't want to speak on behalf of God, but just from what he has observed from being in the range of God's energy for as long as Michael has, war is probably one of the biggest disappointments to Creator God's energy – of everything.

And that's part of why some of Earth's events, like the Great Flood, Ice Ages and so forth were brought forth. Sort of like God was just saying, "Let's start over, let's clean the slate." But part of it, too, was the physiological and biological reaction of the Earth from being the living, breathing entity that She is, and needing to go through massive transformation at various times.

R: The church teaches a lot about self-sacrifice, but Jesus taught that we should love our neighbors as ourselves. This implies that one cannot love his neighbor in a healthy manner unless he has an appreciation and respect for himself. Ayn Rand wrote that we should operate with "rational" self-interest not "irrational" self-interest. This means that for the good of all persons, we should operate to achieve our goals in a manner that does not harm another person. It seems to me that her admonition is consistent with Jesus's teachings.

It follows that the reason these ideas are repugnant to many people is that they do not lead to altruism, where one cannot ever seek self-improvement in any manner without being considered immoral. The philosophy of altruism pervades politics, religion, and sociology, mostly to achieve the transfer of wealth from those who produce it to those who do not. Rand argues that giving to others should be out of desire to do that and not because of moral obligation. I believe Jesus's teaching were the same. He taught a change of heart to want to do good things, and not to act only from fear of retribution. What is your view of these ideas?

C: Back to Raphael, fielding this one primarily; saying that it all tends to harken back to the essence of the Golden Rule, "Do unto others as you would have them do unto you." There are several passages in many spiritual books about loving yourself and treating yourself with respect as not being wrong, but rather necessary to have the proper perspective to care for others. Also, to set an example for them to take the best care of themselves possible by having regard for themselves. So, he says that Rand's writing and teachings are not that far afield, even though she was atheist.

R: I've spoken to her in a previous session with you, and she said she'd always believed that there was a Higher Power, but she wasn't very ecclesiastical about it.

C: She was a great mind, obviously, and part of the cosmic consciousness and The All That Is. She tapped into that truth and felt motivated to write about it. But it is not necessary to be completely self-sacrificing. Poverty does not equal spiritualism. And that's a misconception that many people have bought into through the centuries. Yes, they're saying even Mother Teresa, even though she lived very simply, she knew how to get money out of people to achieve what she envisioned happening.

Gandhi also, even though he was all about peace, he used that example of living so humbly because it was what worked for him. It was what made people give him respect and listen to him.

R: All right, because what he just said was astounding, given the perspective of worldwide conflict, one must address how mankind has chosen to govern itself. There are multiple forms of government including representative democracy, democracy, dictatorship, and kingship, to name the most prevalent.

The Anunnaki are reported to have introduced kingship where the human King was directed by the Anunnaki overseer God. Democracy was probably invented by the Greeks, but it is unknown who first said, "No democracy can last more than 200 years because the citizens would vote for themselves largess from the public treasuryto the point of bankruptcy." The United States and many other countries utilize representative democracy, but that seems to be as fallible as pure democracy, because representatives can be bought.

There are a few kingdoms run by benevolent Kings or Queens, but they do not seem to be the major power players on the world stage, although they're not a threat to anyone. Of those with great natural resources, countries like those of the Arab world have significant economic power, but few share in the rewards of that power. Finally, dictators have always managed to achieve great military power at the expense of enslaving their people, thus threatening others when they run out of money.

Of all these, the ones with the greatest opportunity to do good are the representative democracies where there is a moral basis for the power invested in the government. Even here, there is a temptation to pluck the low-hanging fruit for the well-being of those who do not produce enough for survival or the acquisition of government power for personal use by the representatives and their associates.

So, the truth is mankind has yet to figure out is how to govern itself. Although it might be said mankind has made some headway over the centuries, it seems to me that the teachings of Jesus, if applied, would make any form of government successful and the choice of form could be arbitrary. What do you say?

C: The teachings of the Christ were meant to apply and be presented for consideration by people from all walks of life. However, Jesus had very little respect for governmental authority, as you can well understand, given that they sentenced him to death, even though it was brought up that he was able to outmaneuver that. But there are just too many other diverse cultures and belief systems to create one ruling, and that's part of why the Earth plane is such a conflicted and complex place.

There is contrast so that people can align with either the dark or the light. If there were no contrast, there would be no growth. Jesus would never have said, "My way or the highway," as many of the dictators and other people that you brought to light there have been wont to do. They could learn much from His teachings if they were willing to do so, but that is not to take away from the fact that they could also learn much from the teachings of Buddha, Gandhi, Mohammed, Nehru, or any other wonderful philosophers and teachers and gurus throughout the course of history. Man is wont to strive and to be power-hungry and greedy. Those who can overcome that and walk away from that (getting back to the true authenticity of caring about everyone and not putting themselves above anyone) ... that is the true test, true mark of an evolved soul. Many do not ever achieve this, unfortunately.

The New World Order

R:There's a lot of chatter and claim on the internet that the underlying force causing turmoil in the world is a centrally planned and orchestrated set of actions to put in place by something called the New World Order. This is said to be a tightly controlled regimenting of humans to eliminate the exercise of Free Will outside the realm of central control.

This would seem to be a root cause of dissension and fighting that would be counterproductive to the purpose of the Anunnaki's mission, unless of course all humans acting under Free Will chose to be compliant, which is an unlikely outcome in view of God's purpose in designing in Free Will in the first place. What do you say about this? Is the actual outcome, as you predicted, the failure of all governments to manage anything?

C: They're saying it's more like a part of their intention to not create a world government, but more of a listing or bullet point type of rules to live by type of suggestion. Not a mandate, not a world order; that is part of cabal thinking and Illuminati type of wanting control. They're giving me the feeling that the Anunnaki are going to say something like, "You've got the technology now; if you want non-sentient beings that can carry out certain tasks or do things without arguing, then create robots to do much of that. But don't deprive or enslave mankind from being true to its nature.

Really Bad Things

R: There is reported to be a practice of pedophilia and cannibalism of babies reaching into the highest levels of government, royalty, and the church. It is also said to be widespread in the entertainment world, and to some extent includes Satanic worship. One of the objectives besides pleasure is the extraction of a chemical called adrenochrome from murdered babies. This is reported to enhance appearance well into old age.

There is also an anonymous group of people called "Q" predicted to uncover these practices and their participants, including arrests where laws are violated. First, I would ask if the evil against babies and children is as widespread as reported; and second, is the mission of "Q" as reported, part of the cleansing anticipated by the Annunaki with their culling of mankind into three groups, the third of which is to be removed?

Your commentary on this is important to understanding the widespread forecasting of major change in everything mankind would consider to be part of the fabric of life on the planet.

C: What they're saying here is that people infected with fear are much easier to control, and the term "infected" is used with great purpose here. It's no accident that the world has been infected with this coronavirus concurrently with all these conspiracy theories floating around, because people are already automatically afraid of being exposed to this disease. That just allows their consciousness to be more susceptible to conspiracy theories that are based in fear.

Not to imply that all these theories are not true, because there is truth in a lot of things they're saying. Just think about the number of times that fantastic, seemingly crazy stories have broken first in the tabloids like *The National Enquirer,* and then maybe not immediately but later on down the road, the things that were written about have been proven to be true.

So, it's kind of a camouflage. sort of smoke screen, but it's a manipulation and they're saying that the people behind "Q" are not of the highest intention. Many of them are control mongers.

There have always been atrocities including human sacrifice, and all manner of other devastatingly cruel activities that have taken place on the Earth plane because mankind is vulnerable, and much more so when they have been subjugated to fear.

Part 12: Return of the Anunnaki

Background on Anunnaki History in Science and Metaphysics

R: I previously have taken a DVD course in quantum mechanics and have been motivated to take it a second time, to try to improve my understanding of the conceptual content. It remains difficult and compels a greater understanding and appreciation of the stature of the people who have developed the science and mathematical foundations of this material. In its early days, Albert Einstein referred to Quantum Mechanics as "spooky" because it deviated greatly from Newtonian concepts of determinism where everything was deemed knowable.

In the quantum world of the submicroscopic, nothing is knowable for sure, and everything is probabilistic. I am sure Einstein would recognize now that God does, in fact, play dice with the universe. So now we know that an atom is about a hundred thousand times as large as its own nucleus, and the electrons in orbit are nowhere in particular, but buzz around it in a cloud of uncertainty.

We know that so-called empty space is filled with something we call dark energy, that grows as space expands. The observation of the Higgs Boson shows that there is a field that imparts mass to points of energy known as particles and mass itself is a measure of inertia in a pure vacuum. There is so much more that I do not know, but I believe it is built into the mind or soul to seek to know God by knowing the nature of his creation.

Science pursues knowledge of God in a parallel path to spirituality that chooses a metaphysical approach that appears to focus on seeking to escape the limits of normal physical existence. It seeks to find a direct channel to the world of spirit and therein find God.

Being still, tuning out sensory inputs, and using meditation and prayer are methodological components of the metaphysical approach.

In other words, according to Joseph Selby in his book *The Physics of God,* there is science in the metaphysical approach to seeking God, just as there is religious dedication to the scientific method in the scientific approach. It seems to me that these two branches of endeavor are in the process of stumbling into each other on the same road.

Will they recognize their common goal? How have alien cultures dealt with this? How did the Anunnaki deal with this? I realize I took a circuitous path to get to these questions. but I would appreciate hearing from you on this subject.

C: Interesting! Well, they are reminding me of one of my mentors when I was attending massage school and hypnotherapy school. My anatomy teacher was a very spiritual guy, a scientific medical doctor too, but one of his favorite sayings was, "Science is coming to the rescue of spirituality."

And it feels to me that that's what your question is raising, even though it's maybe more along the lines of religion. But those in spirit are converting that to encompass overall spirituality in general, or "soul understanding," is what they just said; combining that with the knowledge that science has brought about through the ages. So, you were asking, how did alien cultures deal with this?

R: Did they go through the same path where they had a spiritual approach to existence and a scientific approach to existence? And they didn't talk to each other. They were opposites, but actually on the same road.

C: It does feel there were two factions that were split up on those topics among the Anunnaki. While they have been of in this kind of Phantom Zone, or place where they were banished for their misuse of humanity when they were here the first time, they have had greater enlightenment lessons and insights into how to combine the two rather than to look at people as simply tools to manifest what they wanted. They got out of alignment with the original intent that they came here with; they got "drunk with power," is what I just heard someone say.

And if they want to maintain their voice and their presence in the universe, that will never be allowed to take place again... where they get so out of whack with their purpose. It feels there was more of a division the first time that they chose to be here on the Earth plane, during Egyptian times and even prior to that.

R: To broaden that a little bit, do other alien cultures have the same experience of going down the same dual path that eventually joins?

C: Michael says that there are some that are intelligent and aware enough to realize that one really cannot exist fully without the other. Yet there are others that are very cold by nature. He adds, "I don't mean cold temperature-wise, but cold and calculating. They only look at more of the scientific factual aspects rather than combining anything that would be spiritual with that." He says these are more what are classified as the Greys.

Update on Anunnaki Arrival

R: I previously asked for my dad's support to check to see if the Anunnaki have already arrived, and if not, how close they might be to arriving. I realize that this is kind of a burden; he's got to jump through hoops of fire to get permission to ask a question and get the information. The answer is still maybe, "No, they're not here yet." But I just wondered what he knows about it.

C: Well, he says that with some of the sightings that have happened so far with the individual UFOs, part of that has been some of the advance crew or landing party making their way here as initial envoys.

But he says, once the big gathering does take place... you'll know it. Everybody, really, on the Earth plane will know it. (And that's what we were being told about earlier on when we were putting the first book together that they will come in, more of a fleet type of assembly that nobody will be able to write off as an optical illusion or anything like that.) It'll be very clear. But he gives me the sense that is from what he's allowed to see or to share, that's more likely to take place probably somewhere between midsummer and mid-fall. He makes me feel like it would be closer to that time of this year (2022).

R: That's pretty good strong information. That's a better estimate than I expected, that he gave the approximate season.

C: Well, he says, he knows you've been wanting to ask that question. So, I think he's been doing some advanced research.

R: Yes! I thank you, Dad.

C: He says, "Sure. I'm so glad that you are so perennially curious about all this stuff." He adds that it's been a true revelation and education for him to become more involved in the research about these types of things than he was able to do when he was here.

The Road to Dictatorship

R: A third question arises about the nature of population control by governments, leading to dictatorships. We see that recognition and protection of the right to exercise Free Will leads to great benefits to society as individuals and as a whole. Yet there is a propensity to control choices through enslavement to create a shortcut to behavior modification.

Why is the obvious difference so hard to understand and embrace? This seems to be the ultimate test of creation and the primary reason for the ministry of Jesus—to teach mutual love and respect.

C: Michael comes forward and says that part of what is going on in the world today from their perspective with this pandemic, is a very not-so-subtle, but insidious, attempt to control people in ways that the so-called "one-percenters" and others who have always had a thirst and an extreme appetite for power are choosing to enact it. They realize that with the divine feminine awakening more now than in millennia previously, they are kind of running scared. This was a scheme that they came up with to have another way to control people and to inject fear.

But he says the angels feel that ultimately this will fail, and man's desire to be free and to exercise Free Will choice will triumph overall. But this is a dark period in our history right now. He feels that within another couple of years, more factual evidence will come to light that will enable people to start to take their power back.

Learning to Travel the Road to Freedom

R: Because government-controlled societies tend to lead to bankruptcy and war, you have previously noted that we should expect the Annunaki to lead mankind toward free societies as part of the teaching against war.

C: Michael says that is a part of their mission, along with some of the other alien beings that have helped to maintain and course-correct events here on the Earth for hundreds, if not thousands of years. He said chiefly among them, the Pleiadeans have been the peacekeepers to the best of their ability. But he says that is also a big part of the Anunnaki mission. Their ultimate goal is to spread the word of truth and peace, because they will have a very engaged volunteer audience of human beings that are open finally to listening to what they have to share.

Because they caused so many wars when they were here before, this is a big part of their ability or desire to correct that from their last major appearance on the Earth plane.

Part 13: Welcoming

This part brings us to the expected uncertainties of meeting newcomers for the first time and addresses appearance as an example. Our Archangel team gives us a heads up on what to expect and suggests we don't get too excited about differences.

Expectations

R: I am concerned about the appearance of arriving Anunnaki and soon to be revealed aliens since they may be significantly different from humans and difficult to accept.

C: Michael says that if you're most concerned about the appearance of the Anunnaki on arriving, they are more along the lines of human in appearance, but quite a lot taller is the main difference.

R: That's a surprise to me because I've led myself to believe that they are reptilian in nature. If I'm mistaken about that, then it makes a lot of difference in what I have to say in the rest of this conversation. In other words, I don't know whether he is saying that we are more like them or they're more like us in physical appearance without shapeshifting?

C: Yes, that's the information that I'm getting. He says that the Greys, when they reveal themselves, are more of the traditional aliens that we're used to seeing on television and movies with the large head, oversized eyes, no nostrils or just slits for nostrils, and sometimes no mouth. But he says that the race that is headed our way as closer to humans in appearance in general. They can certainly shape-shift if they want to, but the way that they will appear to us is more along the lines of taller humans, like 7 feet tall or so.

R: I've seen a report of aliens making themselves apparent to possibly two or more governments, in particular the Israeli and the U.S. governments. Should we assume that the coming out of hiding is beginning as a warmup to our getting ready for the bigger show to come?

C: Yes, it is sort of a dress rehearsal in a sense to prepare Earth, "earthlings", for want of a better term, to not be afraid or not immediately go on the defensive when the Anunnaki begin to arrive. Some of the councils that are being held between these beings and heads of government are to prepare them so that they don't have a knee-jerk response to the arrival of the Anunnaki, and any other alien life forms that are friendly that may choose to reveal themselves as more time goes by. It's just that this fleet coming in from the Anunnaki is the biggest en masse type of visitation that the Earth has ever or will ever be aware of in such a such a big way.

Adjustments and Integration

R: I may be concerned about something that is not a problem. But history tells us that humans may be quick to see differences and slow to see similarities. This characterization may be related to the age of the human, as younger people may be better at adapting to change since they would have had less time to form firm ideas regarding how things are or should be.

One of the things that is of concern is how the perception of Free Will and resistance to being told what to do will play out against outsiders showing up with instructions on how to do a better job of living. Dealing with this issue involves well-programmed traditions and customs as well as constitutions and legal codes. This is a transition that will take a lot of time, and the business of living will be carried on in some fashion and in parallel.

There will be resistance to changing the form of relationships in many cases because people do not necessarily know what to change and still make a living, for example. History says man adapts, but not necessarily as quickly a central planners would like. How do you see this?

C: Michael is continuing, because he is kind of an attaché or celestial being who has worked with aliens for perhaps the longest of all the Archangels. He says that the rise in the popularity of video gaming has been in some ways a preparatory exercise for human beings to get used to utilizing that not only as a fantasy escape, but also just to program them to be more open. He's talking about not just children, but adult gamers, of course, or ones that started when they were young but are now in their 40s and beyond. It's almost like a flight simulator, but it's more about, "Here's what's going to happen if you press this button."

They can see the consequences of rash action, particularly regarding nuclear and atomic deployment so that there is no guesswork involved, at least not as much as might have initially been of concern during World War II with Hiroshima and Nagasaki.

It's a projection of how things are going to affect the planet forever. He also says more is going to come to light about the devastation that is still ongoing because of various nuclear tests, as well as attacks. That in and of itself should be enough to raise a lot of people's consciousness, to the ones especially who are more in the Green Camp of trying to preserve the Earth. There's hard cold evidence to show them, "Well, if you do this, here's what your results are going to be."

R: Another dimension to the integration of aliens and human society is Jesus's admonition to love one another, which has been addressed previously as meaning something more like respecting one another. When faced with the presence of outsiders, humans tend to find more commonality with those like themselves. This is often described as safety in numbers. It may be that there is a trade-off in using this characteristic of humans to offset the need for shapeshifting to make humans more comfortable with aliens.

It is easier for humans to respect those like themselves than those unlike themselves. It seems the burden of proof is usually on the outsiders to gain respect, and that has to do with having common values with the insiders. This means that the teaching moment may occur when the aliens can convince humans that there is a common set of values that both parties can sign up to.

C: Well, they said you kind of answered your own question. It's very likely that as the trust builds, then there will be a meeting of the minds between the aliens and the humans about creating more common ground that is workable and is understandable and acceptable to both parties.

R: I'm just trying to figure out the intellectual mechanics of achieving large numbers of people... millions or perhaps billions, to change away from the paradigm of warlike behavior to solve problems that seem too difficult to solve rationally. I think it's very complicated to say the least.

Previous Residents

R: Previously you have confirmed that there are up to a thousand aliens in various positions of government around the world. I assume that they either look like humans naturally or have shapeshifted to alter their appearance. It seems to me that there may be a kind of permanent shapeshifting that allows one to look human all the time. Otherwise, there would be difficulty in constantly adjusting to circumstances to hide one's natural appearance.

In any case, the question arises regarding whether the management committee headed by Archangel Michael is planning to orchestrate the coming out of hiding all around the world roughly coordinated with the integration of the Anunnaki into the world scene.

It seems to me the revelation to mankind in the adjustment to the new reality would include an adjustment and possible acclamation to the varied appearance of aliens much as depicted in *Star Wars* movies. Would that be correct? Assuming that, soon mankind's imagination displayed in movies will come to life in reality. A kind of social interchange would seem to be an aide to rehabilitation of mankind to the idea of mutual acceptance and inherent abhorrence of violence. What do you say?

C: Michael says you are on track there, and he says that's interesting. I don't think that he ever brought this up, or any of them have ever really brought this up before, but they say that Rod Serling was a futurist in many ways. Because a lot of the appearances of aliens or strange beings that appeared in *The Twilight Zone* episodes that he wrote were glimpses of the future that he had. Michael's just bringing this forward to say that there is a history of science fiction television and film predating the acceptance of things that are going to just become commonplace in the future.

So, maybe not all the Star Wars configurations of aliens will actually come to life on this planet, but he says George Lucas and also the other scriptwriters who worked on the original trilogy of *Star Wars* had vision and were not just working from their imagination.

Part 14: Alien Direction: What Should We Expect Them to Do?

Human Work Force Focus

R: Is there a plan to convert intellectual and physical facilities focused on making or defending actions of war to more benign enterprises dedicated to enhancing the human experience? I'm thinking of a way to smooth the economic transition away from war to peace without putting a lot of people out of useful work.

This is something that will come to the table almost immediately since so much national effort in most nations is focused on economic issues. I feel sure this issue must have been addressed in other populations that have had to experience this transition, unless of course, we earthlings are the only ones.

C: He says you are not alone in this, but other societies and planetary groups have different views of economic structures, and their own barter system if you will. But he says you make very astute observations, Ray; he commends you on your burning desire to get answers. He's very impressed by the fact that you are so studious and consistent in your quest to get answers to extremely complex problems and situations.

Education

R: I am concerned that the system of educating children and young adults is itself a contaminated process, laced with various agendas that stray from truth in multiple directions. Is there a plan to educate the educators with material that is as close to the truth as sentient beings know how to make it, or perhaps there's a plan to alter the education system in some way not yet imagined by humans?

C: Yes, it feels like a plan is currently in development, and a large aspect of that involves peer teaching. So not the traditional parent-child configuration of teacher-student. It feels this will be the main model in the not-too-distant future; it may involve alien children who have advance knowledge will arrive on Earth to be teachers for our children. They might be maybe four to five years older, but it is more of an aspect of peer teaching and peer mentoring as the old, outmoded model of education is falling by the wayside, or needs to be completely scuttled.

So, there is a plan in the works. It's just not quite ready to be revealed yet, but it should make more sense in the next 5 to 10 years.

Alien Medical Help

R: You've suggested that part of the human dilemma is dealing with infections generated by alien experiments regarding resistance to infection by microorganisms. Would it be reasonable to assume that part of alien intervention in human affairs to calm tensions that might lead to war might include assistance in dealing with infection in general by addressing human immunology? In a more overt way than in the past. I'm thinking of infections that may tend to create paranoia about social and environmental dangers if such infections exist.

C: Yes, he says that's absolutely accurate. With the recent emergence of things such as coronavirus, it feels that the Earth is more attuned and ready to accept solutions from outside sources than it has been up until this point in time. It's almost like these viruses are emerging to in a sense, lay the groundwork for alien intervention to be accepted. Again, it might be on the down-low or hush-hush for a while, but it does feel that proper credit will be given within the coming decade to the alien intervention teams that are doing this for the sake of mankind so that mankind is not wiped out by all of these.

Alien Technological Help

R: I just finished watching a TV series on important technological initiatives to address certain pollution problems, as well as the identification by color of buried landmines. About 100,000 of these are thought to exist. Based on seeding wide areas with a particular plant, the leaves of which change in the presence of buried mines because of the leakage of certain chemicals, buried mines can be located. It seems to me that education of mankind on healing the planet is a good objective.

That is significant; at least locally, that belongs on the agenda with protecting everyone in the galaxy from the effects of nuclear explosions. I'm not suggesting these two are equally important on a galactic scale, but it is important to clean house at home while caring for the surrounding galactic residents. Is there some value in this assessment?

C: "Absolutely!" is what I'm hearing. It was interesting as you're talking about the mines. It feels like there are going to be exploratory teams of both aliens and humans going to some of these locations; they're showing me that it's a matter of the aliens having the understanding and advanced knowledge without needing a lot of instrumentation as Earth scientists tend to rely upon. But just to say, "Okay, everybody needs to be at least a hundred and fifty yards back from this," and they're showing me it's like using some form of laser in their mind; through what we would call their third eye to safely diffuse these things.

That way, there might be a little bit of a "boom," but not nearly as much as if someone were to step on it or detonate it and then disappear in a puff of smoke. It's not as big of a deal because of the way that they understand how to diffuse these; it would be much safer than any way that human beings might try and do this. I feel that there are going to be teams that start closer to home to decontaminate or eradicate many of these potentially harmful devices.

R: They've discovered a lot of children have been killed because they didn't know the mines were in their playground area.

I have been reading a book by Michael Lewis called *The Fifth Risk* wherein he identifies the troublesome project management of managing nuclear waste in the U.S. as the fifth major risk to our proper government. This is based on American stewardship of the monumental nuclear waste burden incurred when the country embarked on the development of nuclear weapons about 80 years ago.

The author focuses on the current administration, and its disregard of the deadly significance of this responsibility. But I see it as a much larger problem of government in general, in keeping the importance of this issue a secret. For example, one important fact was brought up that there is a huge plume of underground radioactivity creeping toward the Columbia River. The end game of that is the poisoning of that river and eventually the Pacific Ocean, and perhaps beyond.

We already know that creeping underground plumes of toxicity must be dealt with promptly lest they poison water supplies. What if all the fish in the river and beyond in the Pacific Ocean became toxic?

As an aside in a previous discussion, Archangel Michael suggested that radioactive waste buried underground is not unrelated to global warming.

This brings me to the upcoming arrival of the Annunaki and their focus on preventing nuclear war by changing the paradigm of human relations. This no doubt springs from a concern about spreading destruction beyond Earth. But I think there is another agenda, and that is to help mankind avoid destroying itself. To that end, it seems to me that an infusion of extraterrestrial knowledge on how to deal with nuclear waste would be not only welcome, but enormously helpful.

Other beings must have dealt with this problem and could bring their knowledge to the table if there was someone there to listen and take heed. I believe that there are such people, but rather than agents of government, they might be scientists and others who have been trying to work the problem. What do you say?

C: Well, it's quite fascinating, because while you're talking, they're showing me pyramids and geodesic dome type of structures being utilized in the near future, quite possibly to create transformative material that can be applied to toxic waste or where the toxic waste could be transported. But it seems that the less it is transported, the better.

It feels like those kinds of geodesic domes, or vibrationally in-tune structures such as the pyramids, have the right configurations to come up with the appropriate material or technology to transmute or disempower toxic waste. Hopefully just to eliminate it safely.

Part 15: Special Topics

Physics: M-Theory

R: This next question is a mind-stretcher. There is a scientific area of thought called M-theory where there are two dimensional branes (short for membranes) that contain holograms of energy that are the domains of initial and continuing creation. If I am not too far off the mark, the holographic projection of one of these branes is the three-dimensional physical universe in which mortals abide.

Another brane may be the hologram of Heaven, and its projection is the Heaven we all have come to know and love. Is any of this true? If not, then thank you for listening. If true, then the question comes to mind as follows: If the hologram of the 3D universe is the blueprint for the structure and function in the 3D physical universe, is there a pairing between the two that reflects Free Will, independent thought, travel, and all actions of all sentient beings in the physical universe? I know this is one of those questions that begs for a treatise on your part. I also know you will succinctly summarize, so fire away.

C: They're agreeing with you that there is a holographic version along with the three-dimensional version, and that is true of many realms in the universe, in that thought and creation often have their genesis or spawning in the holographic realm before it is brought to the 3D realm. Almost as if there were a lab. This is what they're showing me in pictures too, so I'm trying to voice it at the same time. It's almost as if there were a lab of creation where proof of concept takes place before things are brought to the physical world. Then sometimes they must replicate the results before the design of anything becomes tangible and 3D form. I don't know how much this is answering your question.

R: It's right on target. In my reading, I was reminded of how a hologram works. A hologram is really a two-dimensional film that you shine light through, and it creates a three-dimensional entity called the holographic projection. And so, this brane is like the two-dimensional film and the 3D Physical Realm is like a holographic projection. If not an actual holographic projection since we're all energy; everything is energy and then it's not even clear that the concept of matter has meaning except in terms of its resistance to push and pull.

C: They're saying that Einstein, Ben Franklin, and Thomas Edison notably were incredibly inventive personas, but that they all would frequently take naps, not long naps. Maybe just a half hour to 45 minutes.

They would do that not so much to rest the physical body, but to enter this other realm, such as the holographic realm. Then they would take what they learned while in that state and bring it back into the 3-D World. That's how they got downloads a lot of the time, for the inventions that they came up with. They were tapping into that more universal knowledge; almost like going to visit the Hall of Akashic Records and taking a hands-on experiential tour.

They maybe had had the seed for the invention in their mind but didn't quite know how to flush it out yet. They add that a lot of people can travel to this place, and several inventive and innovative people have done that. They're saying Steve Jobs also knew how to do this.

R: Fascinating. Well, this has been overwhelming. I'm motivated to continue research. I hope they continue to be patient with me.

C: Oh, they say that's never an issue. They are grateful that you have such an inquisitive mind and the desire to continue to expand and grow your understanding. They have great love for you.

Brane Theory

R: I would like to engage with the Archangels, if they are available for the next set of questions.

C: I feel them nodding and saying, "Absolutely, go ahead."

R: In a previous conversation you confirmed that there is something like a 2-D hologram utilized by the Creator for planning and proof of concept, and that the 3-D world of which we humans and others are a part is the projection into three dimensions of that planning hologram.

It occurs to me that the hologram construct may be only an analogy since holograms as we know them deal with photons. Photons may not be ingredients of what we refer to as matter, and certainly not of the soul, as that has been said to be of a different material. It seems to me that the hologram analogy deals with projections of the constituents of matter and are therefore much more complex than a simple hologram dealing with photons.

The hologram analogy would have to consider the dynamics of the exercise of Free Will by all participants as well as the ongoing process of creation and would not be a static projection. What do you say about that?

C: Well, they said in your typical fashion you have deduced some absolutely on-track assessments. They say it is a differential number of factors between those comparisons that you just listed. They're not going into great detail, but they made me feel like you are on an accurate track.

R: Thank you for that.

Atlantis Revisited

R: In a prior conversation, I asked about Atlantis and the Kalu and you confirmed that Atlantis had existed, but was destroyed by an inappropriate use by the Kalu of an unusual Earth-centered power source, perhaps thermonuclear. You suggested it might be more suitable to discuss it in more detail at a future time as there was concern that some current entities might try to exploit the same energy source with bad consequences.

So, is it premature to discuss this subject now, or is it better postponed? Also, I recall having read somewhere that escapees from the Atlantean destruction may have settled in islands in the Mediterranean and in the British Isles. If that were true, then might they have interbred with humans?

C: Addressing your last portion of the question first, they say yes, there were some survivors and some escapees, and that part of the world is primarily where they were most able to migrate and find ways to survive. And yes, there was some intermingling of species involved there, just because of scarcity of the survivors. They say survivors of Atlantis probably numbered fewer than 500 people all total, and they were scattered to the four winds, in a sense.

Some were scientists who had essentially done whatever preparation they could because they saw the inevitability of what wound up happening. This was because they were on the inside track of the experimentation that was going on. So, some had prepared, they're saying, not unlike the legend of Superman and Krypton, which was planted in the mind of that superhero's creator... by Atlantean influence.

And as far as talking about the thermonuclear hazard and deployment of that energy source, this is as fine a time as any to talk about it. There are already (they said this is tongue-in-cheek) "underground experiments" going on with it. Now, more and more of these kinds of manipulations of the Earth's core energy are going to be exposed over the course of the next 20 to 30 years so that the public knows more about what's going on.

Possible Error in Locating Israel

R: A Lebanese scholar named Kamal Salibi wrote four books, the first of which is *The Bible Came From Arabia*. In it, he reveals research that leads to the conclusion that when God promised Abraham the land which has been interpreted to be where Palestine is located, that scripture was misinterpreted. and from archeological evidence should have been in Arabia. The outcome of that suggested misinterpretation has been the source of much of the conflict in the Middle East... specifically the location of Israel in Palestine after WWII.

I may be opening Pandora's Box by even bringing this up, but if there is truth in Salibi's work, that might lead to a different approach to solving the regional conflict. Alternatively, it could lead to a worse dilemma. What do you say?

C: They are first acknowledging that this author is a scholar through and through, and has done massive amounts of research, coupled with being an incredibly intuitive soul. They add that first and foremost, many of the books of the Bible were written in either Arabic or Aramaic, and that those two languages are not that far afield from one another. A linguist would understand that better than the average person. Someone who has done an in-depth study of linguistics would understand this similarity that they're referencing.

But as far as the layout of Palestine and Israel and the "Land of Milk and Honey," it feels that more of that initially was referencing ancient Babylon and parts of Iraq and Iran more than modern day Israel and Egypt. These along with other aspects of the Middle East that have also been long involved in conflict. I don't know if that is in alignment with Salibi's research or not, but this is what they offer.

R: I think the essence of Salibi's research was based primarily on the correlation between locations mentioned in the original or earliest biblical texts with existing Saudi Arabian villages in the southwestern parts of Saudi Arabia at a ratio much better correlated than with anything in Palestine.

The Saudi Arabian government may have taken him more seriously than anybody else, because they shut down all archaeological exploration in that region of those designated correlated sites immediately after the publication of his book. At least that's what I've read, right?

C: Archangel Michael is saying, "Yes, he definitely rattled some big cages with that book. And much as Salman Rushdie's writings and poetry were vilified, there are different writers and sharers of alternative truths that governments keep closer tabs on. They're in agreement with you, Ray. That it hit a little too close to home with some of the things that he wrote.

R: Well, if this was true as it has been described, what would be the outcome if people started taking this seriously? The Saudis wouldn't want to give up land. Israelis have established a viable, productive society in Palestine. They're not going to want to pack up their suitcases and move to the desert of Saudi Arabia. Hamas and the Palestinians would say, "It's time for you to leave." This is unbelievably complex. What do you say about that?

C: They say it's not likely to happen in this iteration of the Earth simply because people are such creatures of habit; the current understanding and mindset of people in that part of the world are not likely to be willing to shift and open up to these possibilities. Because there's too much at stake on so many levels.

R: Yes, I think you're right.

Approaching the 4th Dimension

R: One of the ways humans use to visualize the 4th dimension is to produce replicated three-dimensional diagrams spaced apart in a plane with a fourth parameter tracked to cross all the 3D diagrams.

Could this concept be used to build replicated 3D equipment to measure a parameter in the fourth dimension? It seems the interpretation of data collected would depend on how the replicated 3D equipment was placed or connected or when measurement was timed to occur. This question comes from a comment you provided much earlier regarding the possibility of particles appearing for only tiny fractions of time in three dimensions, but residing for longer times in the fourth dimension.

This question does not negate the importance of mass consciousness to achieve general navigation in the fourth dimension but only to open a door to measurement of particles existing in the fourth dimension.

C: I'm hearing that it is possible. It is not up to a prototype stage yet on the Earth plane, but it is something that is being researched and worked toward by different factions of science.

R: Then that's the positive answer I was looking for.

C: And there's something about all of that too, Ray, to do with light and sound frequency. Those two components seem to be very important here with that particular device you're asking about.

What is a Soul?

R: I finished a course on understanding the basic structure and laws of the universe. It explained that the composition of a proton and a neutron is three quarks, which are little, tiny things of specified types. The sum of the masses of these quarks adds up to only 2% of the measured mass of the proton or neutron, so that creates a great puzzle. What's the other 98%?

The conclusion is that the quarks are whirling around inside the confines of the proton or neutron at the speed of light and expending energy. When converted numerically to mass per Einstein's energy mass equation, that adds up to the remaining 98% of the expected mass of the parent particle. The conclusion is that everything we see as matter is really energy. This further implies that there must be a beginning source of this energy and that remains to be assumed or discovered.

Let us assume that is the ever-flowing creative energy of the Creator. This begs the question of the energy of massless soul. In this case, one must assume there are no protons or neutrons to house quarks to buzz around inside; and the energy represented in the entity called the soul is not manifested as matter.

So, the questions are, A: Is the energy of the soul also buzzing quarks but unconstrained to be inside protons or neutrons? And B: Since the soul must be compatible with the physical body and brain of a mortal, must it also be of the same energy form as matter but able to engage for reincarnation and disengage upon death? Lastly, C: Is the soul's energy of a totally different source and form from anything we think we know?

C: Michael is trying to put it into a format that we can understand and in the writing about this, so that others can understand. It's almost like the soul is Saran Wrap, except it's placed inside of the human being when we become physically incarnate. It's like a reverse... instead of the body being wrapped in it, it's wrapped inside of the body and it's not that kind of mass. But that's what he's showing me, and it feels it is comprised of something that we would consider unidentifiable, by and large.

R: It's not made up of quarks and neutrons and protons, it's energy of a different kind, and that's what I really was getting at. It's something totally different than anything we think we know. Massless light? We are told that a black hole looks black because its gravitational field is so strong that light cannot escape.

This seems to conflict with the assertion that souls are beings of light that is presumed to be photons. Since we are told souls are massless light, photons must also be massless and not subject to a gravitational field. But we have measured the effect of gravity on light by observing that light from distant stars is bent as it passes near other high mass objects. The conclusion must mean that souls as beings of light does not mean that they are composed of photons. and that the concept of light in Heavenly terms is different from the concept of light as photons.

This goes back to my opening topic in this session regarding the composition of the soul. It is clearly an energy form of sufficient complexity to process information based on observation, form conclusions, and develop consciousness, values, and relationships.

One can only wonder, what is the medium of this energy form? And is it the same for all sentient beings in the universe with compatibility to the energy form of the Creator so that anyone can sense the presence of the Creator? I do not expect an answer, but I wish I could understand.

C: I'm hearing them say that you think so deeply about all these things; they commend your curiosity and your willingness to learn, always. But the soul is an entity of light that's got to be a different categorization of light. It's obviously very ethereal looking. It's almost like you can't taste it. You can't smell it. You can't touch it with the five senses... that type of light.

It's not like the light that reflects on our hand or a wall from a light bulb or anything else. It's the opposite of the darkness or the heaviness of a gravitational field or of a black hole. It's basically the antithesis of that.

Abortion Law

R: This next topic is quite controversial and involves attempts at legal control of abortion.

First one must ask why some people think abortion is murder of a human being. That brings up the question of what a human being is, and the assumption must be that it is the result of the deployment of a soul into a fetus that has manifested signs of life.

So, there must be two components, the presence of a soul and signs that the fetus is alive. One governmental entity defines life as the presence of a detectable heartbeat and makes the unstated assumption that a soul was deployed, installed, or injected into the fetus by some means. This latter presumption is that at some prior point a soul becomes associated with the fetus, and from that point on a human being exists. Therefore, to abort the pregnancy is the killing of a human being. This set of presumptions codified into law makes abortion a felony.

How does this scenario play with the mother's Creator-endowed Free Will? The bottom line eventually concludes that she should not have been willingly involved in sexual intercourse if she did not accept or acknowledge the risk of becoming pregnant. (Most laws exempt victims of rape from the legal terms). While that conclusion may hold some truth, the question is whether she should be punished, and whether anyone assisting in an abortion should be automatically punished.

From another viewpoint, one might consider that a spirit may have chosen to reincarnate into that fetus and in the case of abortion could reconsider and redeploy elsewhere. In that case there would be no crime. Going one step further, one might consider that the Creator chose to deploy a new soul into that fetus and in the case of abortion the Creator would no doubt have the undeniable skills to redeploy that soul elsewhere. In that case there would be no crime.

To assert or assume that redeployment is unavailable would be something of an insult to the Creator. It is true that many women have emotional consequences from having abortions, but it seems to me to be devoid of criminality.

I think the whole concern stems from a belief, perhaps misguided, that sexual pleasure for any reason other than procreation is immoral. And that may be incorrectly credited to the Anunnaki males who took human wives, as recorded in Genesis.

I have presented my views based on a somewhat procedural approach to the incorporation of a soul into a fetus; but I do not know how to express that procedure in the more astounding manner by which it is accomplished. For that I ask forgiveness.

Please correct my thinking and conclusions as appropriate.

C: Raphael says that there really is no need for correction because you have essentially hit the nail on the head. In the Creator's eyes as well as in the angels', who as you know, are extensions of the Creator, that there is no crime. That it does in some cases, hearken back to the Anunnaki as you mentioned, but it really got out of control as the Catholic Church began to formulate more and more rules and regulations regarding conception.

He adds that sadly, the manipulation that has been done, the attempted brainwashing and successful brainwashing, in fact, of many of the followers of that religion, was based upon greed and wanting more people to grow up in that faith and keep the church afloat financially. That's where it all stems from initially.

Then there are others that have even more insidious motivations to control others' actions, and part of that does harken back to alien intervention and wanting to utilize humans more as a set of convenient puppets that they manipulated according to their own whims and desires.

But as far as the Creator is concerned, from what we know and understand, you are absolutely correct. You cannot kill a soul, for they are eternal. Once they have been birthed, whether on the other side, as all souls tend to first generate, or once they die here on the Earth plane, they can continue on. So that's a very astute assessment that you've concocted and certainly one that does not require any kind of forgiveness.

R: Thank you.

Christianity: Wrong Emphasis?

R: In previous conversations, I have summarized my understanding of the life of Jesus, based on various documentation and ultimately confirmations of this understanding from Heavenly sources. I remain bothered by the simple statement that Jesus did not die on the cross but was spared human-declared death by his uncle Joseph of Arimathea administering a drug to him. I would like to address that issue in more detail.

First, if there were such a thing as a checklist for human death, and one had to experience all elements of that list to qualify as being dead, then I believe there is not an issue that Jesus experienced all the elements of that list. That means that He suffered the experience of that list. One of the things not on that list is recoverability.

We in the Earth plane frequently learn of the so-called miraculous recovery from being declared dead to being alive. Sometimes fully alive and sometimes alive with disabilities, but nonetheless alive. So, it is not incorrect to say that we can be aware of a person's declared death and be also aware of that person being recovered to an alive state?

It seems to me that the Christian doctrine of Jesus having suffered, bled, and died is not negated by His recovery, although that has been interpreted to be a Divine miracle. That same sort of miracle is a frequent event witnessed without so much as a mention of God (i.e., someone dying on the operating table, but then coming back to life). Full credit is given to modern medical technology that is assumed to have sprung unaided from the mind of man.

In view of these observations, it seems to me that the issue of Jesus's recovery from the dead by whatever means is no more important than the issue of the severity of his suffering... whether for mankind's sins or just existing to teach the amazing apparently unacceptable doctrine of loving your fellow man and treating others as you would like to be treated.

This means that the meaning of Jesus's life is dependent much less on His death and resurrection and much more on His teachings. That, it seems to me, should be the message of Christianity.

What do you say?

C: It's interesting, because they were conferring as you were talking and saying these are a series of very in-depth questions. We've got Raphael and Michael at the forefront here. One of the things that I heard them saying was that what Joseph of Arimathea administered to Jesus was very similar to the same type of root or herb extraction that Shakespeare referred to Juliet taking in *Romeo and Juliet* to give the appearance of being dead, but that she would awaken after a period of time.

So, it basically anesthetized Christ to a degree so that he did not experience the full pain of the crucifixion. Christianity has blown that suffering out of proportion to incite guilt in the followers of Christianity; and you're right that His teachings were His purpose, not that His death be glorified.

Also, He knew that He would never be out of the spotlight or allowed to live any kind of "normal" life following that experience, that crucifixion. Therefore, they came up with this plan to have Him come back to life or, as Christians have called it, be resurrected.

They're saying He already was married to Mary Magdalene in the eyes of God... they were husband and wife. This was kept hidden from the general public, due to her past history and to protect His reputation from being tainted. But they were able to escape and have a normal life after this.

The other thing that they pointed out to me was that a lot of the crucifixion was done through holographic projection to convince the people that were there witnessing it; that it was really happening in the way that it wound up being recorded in Biblical history.

They're comparing it to the illusion of 9/11 of the planes flying into the towers being partially built upon holographic constructs.

That's interesting, because I've heard that in conspiracy theories before but they're affirming that this can happen. It's a sort of mass hypnosis that can take place.

R: Are they saying that what we did see in the videos of the buildings being hit by the planes was a holographic presentation, or just that it could have been?

C: They say that more is going to come out on this within the next five to seven years. There's going to be some actual factual documentation of that very thing. They add, "We don't want to tip the hat too much here, but the planes were definitely not what detonated the destruction of those towers. There were bombs that had been placed in the towers."

R: Wow! Looks like I've uncovered Pandora's Box here on one issue. They have straightened me out on a couple of things here, one about the drug and the reference to Juliet and Shakespeare's play, and eventually validated that my roughly correct assumption about the emphasis of Christianity. I asked a simple question, and I got an education.

C: I never know where they're going to go with this stuff, that's for sure. It's very enlightening to me, too.

R: Thank you for that.

Man's Standing as a Player

R: Is it not true that a rational perspective would be helped by learning to differentiate between those who are messengers of "The All That Is" and other created sentient beings we call aliens? Has that differentiation not been made extremely difficult by the fact that there are aliens whose powers exceed man's ability to comprehend much less ignore? How are we supposed to tell the difference?

C: It is different, and it is difficult. It is not meant to deceive or to trick others, but the alien beings that began migrating and then disclosing themselves to Earth's inhabitants going back as far as about 7,000 BC at least, appeared in different ways. They appeared before humankind with a cognizance of the Angelic realm, and they appeared by their own Free Will. Therefore, it's up to the individual who has this connection with them or with revelations or messengers from the angels to trust their discernment to know who they're interacting with.

Raphael is chuckling and saying, "Cheryl has always known beyond the shadow of a doubt when one of us is speaking. Other people may try and pick that apart and say she just wishes it was them, but it is her conviction in knowing." It is the same pretty much with everyone else. Even if they're not absolutely sure and have no scientific proof as to who it is, it's a matter of their discernment to say, "This is who I was working with."

They're comparing it to *A Course in Miracles*, whose author was certain that Jesus was giving her information to turn into that text.

Precious Metals and Their Roles

R: In past meetings, I got the impression that you Archangels were not impressed with Earth people's affinity for precious metals, such as gold, as a form of money. This is a puzzle since precious metals can't be counterfeited. Unsupported paper money and the mismanagement of paper money by the world's central banks is at the root of the collapse of governments and monetary systems. I believe that there's a functional need for an efficient medium of value and trade so some form of money will arise, but printed money is cheap to produce and becomes a tool for those wishing to create the illusion of wealth without producing anything useful.

Could you clarify what you think we're supposed to do in the face of the disaster produced in this area? I'm referencing when gold was abandoned as a basis of monetary value for individual citizens allowing the governments to fake financial success with paper money, while reserving gold for International Exchange?

C: They're saying that the precious metals (gold and silver being the two most prominent ones) ... The reason they tend to not to overemphasize the importance of them as a monetary means is because they look at them more as fuel. That's why a lot of aliens have traveled to the Earth and other places, to seek gold for its energetic properties, rather than to amass it simply to say, "Look how wealthy I am."

But it does feel that there will become more of an esoteric sort of monetary exchange. It's an energetic value to trade for what someone has to offer in exchange, almost like a barter system. Such as, "I have this skill that I can offer," and somebody assigns a denominational amount to that.

It does seem that the paper money is going to fade out and there may well be some sort of gold or precious metals flaking done to what they're showing me is more like coins or almost more like marble... something that's a spherical source of money. It's something that we haven't seen yet obviously, but maybe in previous cultures, a cruder representation of that in past cultures. They're saying it's something like Wampum, along those lines.

But rather than gold coins or bars... it might have an energetic infusion of that, but a lot of it is just the value of what a person brings with their skills to the table. They're showing me it might make a lot more sense within the next 10 to 15 years.

R: That would be quite a long time after the Anunnaki come in 2022; that seems to be a conflict. It seems to me like the Anunnaki are going to shake us up if we haven't already shaken ourselves up.

C: Maybe it's just an unknown at this point.

R: More astounding is their statement that gold could be used for fuel.

This is so antithetical to Earth science that my mind is boggled by this. Because if I remember my chemistry correctly, the outer electron ring of a gold atom has got eight electrons in it, and that makes it what's called an inert metal element. It does not react with anything as a matter fact. Aqua Regia, the solvent made of nitric and sulfuric acids is the only thing that will dissolve gold, and it'll dissolve pretty much everything else too.

So, I am puzzled about what they're thinking. Maybe some chemistry that we haven't stumbled onto yet because if gold were suddenly useful for fuel, we would be in big trouble. I don't think there's that much of it.

C: What they're showing me is the pyramids, and the value that the Pharaohs, Egyptians, and other ancient cultures placed on gold was an energetic sort of fuel that emanates off it. We may not be aware of this now, and nothing recently on the Earth plane has been rendered tangible or visible to us. It's not so much the melting and burning up of the gold, but the energy that can arise from it, or be gleaned from it somehow.

R: It may not be a chemical reservoir of energy. It may be electromagnetic, but that is alien to anything we know about this. That's revolutionary.

Population Management

R: There is angst among knowledgeable humans about population growth. Is this problem in need of worldwide birth control? In past wars and plagues, not to mention starvation, have kept the population manageable. That does not appear to be viable for the long run, given technological advances in all areas. It seems there are two obvious paths: worldwide birth control in the short run, and extra planetary colonization in the long run. What is your assessment?

C: Worldwide birth control is an excellent concept, but one that is virtually impossible to enforce. The colonization of some of these Earth-like planets recently discovered by astronomers can happen, but again that is in the future. They're saying maybe at least two centuries, perhaps not that long, is what I'm hearing. Or it could happen even sooner; just depends on Interstellar cooperation for transportation to those places using some of the wormholes and other portals that we have discussed in previous sessions.

This would be so that the people they transport are not already senior citizens by the time they arrived. They're saying worldwide birth control is a high-end concept in a low-rent world. The evolution of that being widely accepted is sketchy at best.

R: Doesn't seem like at the current rate of explosion of the population we could last 200 years without starving to death to get the ride to the next planet.

C: It feels that they are going to be more disasters of various kinds that do wipe out significant amounts of world population. They're saying that is not necessarily with the exclusion of some warfare; hopefully not, but that that could be a pathway. They're also talking about the Illuminati's hidden agenda as far as trying to reduce the population via covert means that are sometimes right in front of one's face.

Michael is showing me chem trails in the sky. I have felt for some time and my guides told me those are a machination of the Illuminati, creating airborne illness to try and quietly control us or create sickness to the point that many people are wiped out. It hasn't become overly aggressive thus far because they are trying to keep it under wraps. He says it will play out the way it does with all the people and minds that are involved hopefully coming to some sort of peaceful resolution. But right now, the exact outcome is unknown.

R: Previously you have suggested that colonization of another planet may be part of the solution to excessive population of this planet. In a course I am taking on microorganism adaptation and human co-adaptation to environmental change, I am reminded that humans are very concerned about infecting another planet with human-borne organisms during exploration of that planet. Little is mentioned about existing microorganisms on the alien planet infecting human explorers.

However, I am sure that is and should be a major issue of concern. To that end, your suggestion that robotic entities manufactured on Earth may become commonplace in the not-too-distant future suggests that early exploration of alien planets may be by such robots or androids, or other inorganic entities not vulnerable to organic infection.

It seems to me that this use of inorganic units is the surest way to avoid infecting the Earth with more alien microorganisms brought here by returning astronauts, as well as minimizing the risk of infecting another planet with Earth's microorganisms.

Perhaps it also should be an objective to delay placing humans on an alien planet prematurely, at least until inorganic units have rendered the target planet a minimal risk. What would be your advice?

C: Michael is giving you like a big thumbs up, saying that you have deduced some very accurate potential as far as how this might become reality. He said there definitely are scientists already exploring the possibility of utilizing some of the drone technology to do some of that exploration you're talking about. But this is taking it to a different level... not quite to the Hubble telescope level, but inorganic explorers that can deliver accurate samples of other planets' soil samples, light samples, etcetera, where humans could not sustain the exposure or would pick up and bring back when they return to Earth. So, he says you're really on a solid foundation with that theory.

Genetics

R: It is claimed that humans have decoded virtually all the human genome. I have my doubts about that. I'm not sure this is accurate. What do you say?

C: He says, "We're with you, Ray. Unfortunately, people's egos like to take credit before it's really due."

R: So, is it possibly true that some human characteristics are dependent upon a large array of genes, some of which remain a puzzle, rather than the very few believed by the geneticists?

C: Absolutely. And that would also make a great deal of sense. With all the different alien iterations and interracial, if you will, concoctions of beings that have been created through various expeditions to mate with humans and create a new race, science just doesn't have all the equipment to delineate all of that to an exact degree.

R: I have read that all humans share the same genetics to the extent that we are 99.9% the same, leaving only one part in 10,000 to differentiate us physically.

Assuming this is true, there are still differences based on behavior, values, practices, customs, language, and perhaps a host of other things that comprise what we would call the soul or mind of the person. Some of these differences could be ascribed to geography or environment, including interaction with other human cultures. But are all major differences to be ascribed to whatever Anunnaki person oversaw the humans and what rules he or she set up? Furthermore, have other aliens been primarily responsible for some isolated human cultures?

C: Yes, other cultures have also had a hand in that sort of diversity. And the Anunnaki master, or whoever was calling the shots, type of thing.

R: Yes, they assigned family members, children, grandchildren, nieces, nephews, etc. to run various city states around the world. Those beings were not truly well-equipped to govern, and they made rules according to whatever they thought was right.

C: Basically, nepotism running wild, isn't it? I just heard Michael say that was because they didn't trust any other race or purebred race. That's why they tried to control it that way. He says you've got a good handle on all that, Ray.

Ethics

R: Until the 1970s there were three ethical systems defined and practiced in Western civilizations. First, there is the Ethic of Absolute Right and Wrong. Second, the ethic of doing the greatest good for the greatest number is called the Utilitarian Ethic. Third is the Ethic of Rights, forbidding actions to initiate harm to another person.

In the 1970s, a fourth concept was introduced and that is of Caring For One Another. The complete set of ethics is subsumed under Jesus's admonition to love one another, but the Greeks had a word for each kind of love. I ask if what Jesus meant might be better understood to be to respect one another with empathy? Your comments would be extremely valuable.

C: Raphael says you're on the right track with that regarding respect, because that is indeed a major component of love. Jesus was not just giving a blanket suggestion to love as to gather to one's bosom and hug and kiss and give demonstrative physical love; but to love the whole being. And that does include a sense of mutual respect and ability to allow someone's greatest gifts to shine. To encourage one another in that, they say, is more of a comprehensive overview of what they believe Jesus meant.

The Word

R: The Chinese word "Tao" refers to the fundamental path or glue that ties together the fabric of existence and is synonymous with the Greek word "logos" and the English translation "word." It is written that Jesus said He is the Word, and that if we follow Him, we will find Heaven. Yet you have said all sentient beings are welcome in Heaven unconditionally.

Further thinking on this subject seems to imply that Jesus was speaking more in terms of the Tao than the path of adherence to the Christian religion, which seems to have grasped Jesus's statement as an indication of the uniqueness of Christianity. Is this rendering of the Word as a paradigm of existence a better understanding of Jesus's intent, and a reflection of His Oneness with the Father?

C: I'm hearing, "Yes indeed, that is so. How people decide to create a religion and then what to name a religion is often based upon the name of the iconic person or individual, such as Buddhism, Lutheranism and Christianity. We make it all about other things. We have created religion to justify wars and everything right on down the line... 'Ours is better than yours.' But there only is One Source, One God called by many names."

Nuclear Energy Transfer

R: In earlier discussions the inference has been made that the energy transfer among planets due to nuclear detonations is ultrasonic. I'm keying on that word "ultrasonic", and I could be wrong about that. It is a puzzle since it is assumed there is no medium to carry energy of any sonic nature at any frequency in extradimensional space. That seems to beg for clarification. Maybe I misunderstood how that energy gets transferred?

C: Gabriel is stepping up here now. He's talking about the concepts of two things, mainly reflection and refraction. He says reflection, of course, has more to do with light energy and refraction has to do with the bending of light when it goes to a different medium. He's showing me a kaleidoscope as you turn its wheel while looking through it... it changes form. But then he says there's one final click and it's all black, so there's nothing left to look at. There is a transmission of energy on different levels in different locations.

God Has Time

R: I've just finished reading a book containing Stephen Hawking's ideas on the answers to the big questions. His argument is that God could not have initiated the Big Bang because there was no time prior to the Big Bang during which God could have initiated creation. This argument is not satisfying to me given that time is described as something of an abstract human construct to explain the distance between events. But I'm not qualified to argue the point.

I have taken a DVD course on the cosmological study of time, which may make me smarter, but because Hawking is now with you in Heaven, I respectfully suspect his view of things in general is evolving.

Few humans have the conceptual skills on arrival there to continue exploring with the energy Hawking has demonstrated in the past. I can only wish him well in his path to continued discovery. I wish to be developed enough to learn from him and others like him. I was deeply moved by his insight into the future on several issues, including artificial intelligence and its promises and risks.

I hope when I arrive at the Heavenly domain, I can be afforded a visit with this man as well as others described as Ascended Masters.

C: Yes, I hear them saying that that can assuredly be arranged because a large part of Stephen Hawking's insistence that there was no God has to do with what happened to his physical self... what he went through with disease. Yet they're saying one of the main questions (they're not saying it definitely has been, because his life review is something privy to him and his guides) but they're saying we suspect that one of the first questions that he has had to tussle with since migrating here is, "How then do you explain your staying alive for as long as you did with a disease that tends to take people almost immediately following diagnosis? Typically, within three to five years, and yet you lived with it for decades? What source do you attribute that to?"

R: When I read his book, it contains so many references to God that I believe he had evolved away from atheism. I had a similar reaction with Ayn Rand when I spoke with her in a reading we did, because she was supposedly a devout atheist. But she said she always believed in a Higher Source, and I think he probably experienced that same thing.

C: I get the sense that a lot of self-proclaimed atheists really are more agnostics who have had horrible experiences with one church of the other, but they remain anti-religious, which is not the same as being atheists.

Time Travel

R: I have taken two courses that discuss the physics of time travel, and the Earth scientific community predicates their logic on the concept of travel to the past on the assumption that action will be taken to alter the future. This leads to logical paradoxes that make such travel impossible but totally ignores the alternative of travel to the past as an observer taking no causative action.

Earlier when I mentioned that Ambar Anati traveled back in time to have a conversation with Mary Magdalene, the wife of Jesus, regarding events after His crucifixion, I mentioned that she, Victoria, went to the Hall of Akashic Records and was outfitted with a translation device to allow her to hold a conversation with Mary Magdalene.

You confirmed that that was one way of solving the language problem, but you did not indicate that the backward time travel was impossible. You indicated that travel to the past as an observer was to be an expected possibility. In this case there was only an information exchange about the past and no indication that any causative action was taken or could have been taken.

So, the question is whether a time-traveling observer taking no action preserves the logical order regarding altering the future? This issue comes up in the logical analysis regarding information transfer between the present and past regarding a message pertaining to the future. I think the last sentence may answer the question, because action is expected to be taken in the past to alter information in the future and that would be forbidden.

Am I confused or is information transfer not considered an alteration of the future? Is it not true that Ambar Anati did nothing to alter the future but only revealed the past? Is revealing information about the past to the future considered to be altering the future?

C: Delivering information to beings existent in the present timeframe that future visitors are visiting then depends upon the Free Will of those who receive the messages. It's not so much laid at the feet of the messengers themselves. It's interesting, because they're showing me kind of a retrospective of different shows and different books by Ray Bradbury and other sci-fi authors that have dealt with time travel.

Is the Universe Friendly?

R: In our entertainment business, particularly in science fiction, much of the plot depends on mankind's ventures bringing them in contact with adversarial forces creating combat situations. This seems to revisit man's tendency to war. Are these scenarios realistic, and are there a lot of war-like species in the universe? Or is the universe more benign and in keeping with the spirit of the Creator? In the past you have suggested that there are very advanced civilizations that think they are so intelligent as to not need any spiritual guidance or motivation to comply with Heavenly purpose. Can you comment?

C: Michael says there is a range of different levels or forms of intelligence. Some very much left to their own devices, like man or hybrids that are human mixed with alien intervention.

There are some that will be very selfish, and the science fiction franchise in the entertainment world was in its beginnings mythological, carrying forward some of the alien interaction that was going on in ancient times. That was very violent in some cases. But a lot of those aliens were disguised or masked as human beings or humanoid beings, to be able to exercise their power more readily.

If they had just come to Earth, as in a movie like *Independence Day* or some of the other *Star Wars* or *Star Trek* alien civilizations and shown such aggressiveness, then they would have virtually destroyed the entire human race altogether.

But a lot of sci-fi writers know, much like Joseph Campbell taught about the need for heroes, that there needs to be conflict that can be overcome ultimately in order for audiences to feel uplifted or encouraged to believe that good triumphs over evil. Michael says he doesn't know if that exactly answers your question or not. But he says, yes, there are good and bad, light and dark, good and evil... whatever you want to term those. By and large, the angelic feeling is that most alien beings are certainly open to creating more of a cooperative existence in the universe.

R: That's a satisfying answer because one can't help but wonder if the Anunnaki turn us into to a pacifist society, and if we decided to work the population problem with exploration to other planets, it's good to know that we have a higher probability of running into help than danger.

C: Yes, absolutely.

Wisdom vs. Knowledge

R: A recent telecast reminded me of the sometimes-vast difference between knowledge and wisdom. In our many conversations I have been seeking truth mostly in the form of knowledge but lingering in the back of my mind is the concern whether access you have given me to the knowledge buried in the questions and answers also is wise to provide to readers because of the consequences that may cause trouble.

I assume you have been providing and will continue to provide guidance in this issue. We are challenged to be messengers and as such, it is our aim to deliver the message as provided. Thank you for the opportunity to be of service. We aim to please.

C: They say, "We send gratitude and blessings back to you as well."

Part 16: Persona

This section includes conversations, however brief, with Zechariah Sitchin and Ayn Rand, who chose to respond to my request for an audience.

Also, it covers my question about why no one with whom I spoke mentioned having sought or received an audience with Jesus. Archangel Michael explains.

Other famous people and beings are also addressed.

Famous People

R: (Speaking to Sharon) I start with, "Have you seen Jesus?" And was I correct that you

Have studied art over there under Monet or Manet?"

C: She says as far as seeing Christ, it's more of the feeling that He is present everywhere, and it's just more palpable in Heaven than it is on the Earth plane. But she says, "I can see Him, I can catch a glimpse of Him; He is just sort of everywhere over here. But the same is true of other great teachers and Masters." She's showing me Buddha, Mohammed, Gandhi, Mother Teresa, and teachers like that.

She says to you, "Honey, it's sort of like this: they're in a separate sort of dimension. The dimensions are all connected, but it's almost like they are off in a conclave, some of these very evolved beings that meet and spend more time together. But they do walk among the rest of us here, too."

She adds, "It's not that they're trying to keep separate from us, but they deal with things that they do require seclusion. I understand that, but I always have such a strong sense of comfort and peace that Jesus and God are just everywhere. It's so much more peaceful here; there's no war, of course, no dissension. I do sometimes attend meetings where we pray for the Earth plane, because it still needs all the help it can get. We worry about our loved ones there about the Earth itself. Sometimes that's where it's more likely that these beautiful teachers and leader energies will show up."

The artist under whom Sharon studied watercolors was Monet.

R: Zechariah Sitchin wrote about 7 or 8 books about the beginning of mankind on the planet. He was an expert in cuneiform writing, and he applied that expertise to translating stone tablets found in what is now Iraq.

In Genesis it talks about the Anunnaki (aka Nephilim) being on the Earth in early days. Sitchin wrote extensively about the Anunnaki's adventures here, and apparently God or God's agent told them to get off the planet about 500 B.C. because they messed everything up so badly. Now, my question for him is, "Do you know any more now than you did when you were here?" (Laughter)

C: He's saying, "It would be impossible not to. It would be like burying your head in the sand."

R: Is he communicating with you right now?

C: Yes, I feel that because of your connection to his books, the link between you is strong. While you were talking about that, I felt like he was saying, "Absolutely, I know more here."

R: He may know more; does he know different?

C: Yes, he says, "If I were on the Earth plane again, and I may be," – I guess he's considering coming back – he says, "I would write with a less heavy-handed style."

Maybe he's thinking he was very adamant about many things. But he's just learned to accept and understand more. I haven't read any of his stuff, so I can't speak for myself, but I feel there was a lot of truth in what he wrote.

R: His first book was called *The Twelfth Planet,* and you may find that an exciting read.

This next question may be unacceptable because I don't really know the person. My most respected author was Ayn Rand, and while she was not engaged in any kind of religious activity when she was here, she seems to me to be an extremely spiritual person. I'm just curious, because she was a great thinker, is she in discussions with other great thinkers and philosophers as part of her Heavenly involvement?

C: It's fine to make a request of anybody's Higher Self, and usually in the case of someone who was famous, they realize the reason you're inquiring is because you were an admirer and that their life's work touched you in a significant way.

She says, "I would never have been a member of the round table at the Algonquin like a lot of my fellow writers when I was on the Earth plane because even some of them over here still don't get me. But it doesn't mean I don't enjoy some of the things they wrote – they had great minds in their own right, and a lot to share, gifts to convey to the world." It's not disparaging in any way on her part to say that, not disrespectful, but she was always considered kind of eccentric, she says, or an oddball, by her fellow writers, her contemporaries, when she was here.

R: I believe that to be true.

C: She said she did always feel a deep and abiding connection with a Higher Power; that there is a reason we are all here, even though in her writing, she says she did sometimes get carried away with a lot of detail, that obviously someone such as yourself didn't mind. And she says there are others that she knows who enjoyed that.

It's interesting – she says in some ways she looked at detail through her own eyes, almost like a camera viewfinder – taking detailed pictures of all kinds of things in any environment that she would go into, as well as detailed investigation into the characters' souls and minds that she created. But she says, "I wasn't an atheist pure and simple by any means; I knew there had to be some kind of Higher Power...higher intelligence."

She was more comfortable calling it that. She tried to inspire people to reach within themselves – if she was able to do that and tap into their own greatness in whatever way possible, then she did her job well.

R: Well, extend my thanks to her for talking to me.

C: Yes. She says, "You certainly have a fascinating way of perceiving life, Raymond, and great thinkers ask intelligent questions rather than just spouting off their own dogma." (Chuckles) So she admires the fact that you take the time to ask such thoughtful questions.

R: In my case, I have been privileged to get special audience with wise and knowledgeable beings such as Michael, Raphael, and Gabriel plus others whose names I do not know, through no credit to myself. This gift has been due to Heavenly respect for Cheryl, my friend and benefactor. Is there a similar relationship in Heaven available to those abiding there?

C: They're showing me it's almost the equivalent of changing the channel with a remote control here. Their Consciousness is that far advanced in those higher Dimensions that they simply think or mind-meld for... trying to put it into terms that we have heard here on the Earth plane through sci-fi and through other types of entertainment.They say it's a little more advanced than that, but it's a way that we can grasp it. But yes, they can do the same thing with more ease than we can, usually.

R: Since there is so much opportunity in Heaven for personal growth in knowledge and service, and the willingness to partake of that opportunity is so much a personal choice, then that would account for a vast difference in how people deal with their own existence and sense of value. Do counselors and spirit guides operate based on their own initiative or some higher directive? Or do they read the readiness of individuals to get assistance in planning a personal growth path?

C: Again, I'm hearing there's a combination of that; they basically volunteer to have that teacher or mentorship relationship, and it can go both ways. For example, there are those on Earth that pray for advanced knowledge or spiritual elevation. They feel that these Heavenly counselors and teachers, basically say, "I choose this one and that one," whereas there is that two-way street, where the Earthly beings can also say, "I wish to work with so and so."

It can go both ways, but it's usually easier for most human beings to believe that they have been chosen rather than to seek out a specific teacher or mentor.

Jesus

R: I previously asked if anybody had seen Jesus. I got a couple of answers back that He hangs out in a separate sort of conclave or dimension or place or existence... He's out and about occasionally and people see Him from a distance, but I don't hear anybody say they've asked for an audience, or that they were denied an audience; that they were told not to ask or anything like that. I am just curious, given all the religious teaching that we've all undergone here, why has that not come up? Is it forbidden? Is it just not kosher, or what?

C: (LAUGHS) No, I don't think it's any of those things. Let's see how the Angels respond. Archangel Michael is the main one fielding this one. I have had Jesus's consciousness come through in readings before, but more frequently Mother Mary's, whom I have trance channeled several times. Michael is telling you, "Nothing is really forbidden, but much as the Christ taught when He was there on Earth, everyone there and in this dimension has that birthright of Divine purpose, that creative spark within them."

And that's what Jesus taught – He never wanted anybody to be completely dependent upon Him. He went through such an intensive interaction with people in His last incarnation that He just hopes that the remnants of His teachings, especially the Golden Rule... be kind to one another is enough to hold people over. Just to help them know that they can do all the things that He did and even greater. But a lot of people here on Earth forget that He ever said those words. But they're in the New Testament.

It's not forbidden to have an audience with Him or anything like that, but more of an awakening that Christ consciousness inside of everyone, more than Him giving Sermons on the Mount or anything like that in that dimension. He's kinda been there, done that.

R: Everything you're telling me is consistent with what I heard early on from Sharon and everybody else. I asked the question, "Do you feel the presence of God, or do you sense God?" and I was told that His presence is felt everywhere.

C: Right.

R: And that's what I'm hearing from Michael?

C: Yes. And this is what I've believed for a long time, too, that a lot of the Ascended Masters or consciousness teachers, such as Jesus, Buddha, some of the saints and so forth...they don't necessarily band together but are more in a similar realm with one another a lot of the time. But it's not that they are not accessible to everyone else. They certainly are. It feels like their mission when they were here on the Earth plane was pretty much achieved; now that information can be tapped into by people in that dimension as well as those who are here. We just tend to use it more as a crutch here on the Earth plane.

R: Yes, and I appreciate this dialogue, because it clears up a lot of subtle mysteries.

And it's emancipating in its nature.

Heavenly Beings: Angels

R: This question is for Sharon – is your spirit guide that works with you there the same person as your previous Guardian Angel when you were still here? How do you experience that person? Mentally, visually? Who initiates contact, that sort of thing?

C: She is saying that Guardian Angels are a special category, pretty much assigned to protect people on the Earth and in other dimensions, too, from a higher perspective. They are often not simultaneously spirit guides; they move on to the next client, so to speak, once a soul that they have been working with has migrated into the Light. She adds that there are different categories of Angels and spirit guides, just like there are different levels of grade school, middle school, high school, university teachers and professors.

R: Are Archangels Michael, Gabriel and Raphael working and abiding in the same dimension? And in how many dimensions do they have capability to complete their function? Does the scope of their responsibilities extend beyond Earth-related people?

C: Yes, beyond those here on the Earth, I feel that is a true statement. Again, I'm getting this, "18 levels of hierarchy," but that they are primarily involved in the lower 13...this is new to me, too, Ray, I've never read this anywhere, to my knowledge, anyway... I like it when you ask these detailed questions because it's always revelatory to me in some way, too. But they're saying their primary guardianship is to the Earth, and not just humans, but for other creatures that need their assistance and support and help. There are also animal angels and evolved spirit beings.

They're saying that there's a reason that Ganesha, Loki, and all these animal gods, especially a lot of the Egyptian ones showed up – they existed, and their spirit still helps the animal kingdom. But the Archangels can travel or migrate between these full 18 levels, kind of as messengers from the top 5 on down into these lower 13. But their primary guardianship does consist of human beings.

R: How do Angels perceive the will of God? Does it come through one of the management councils, or is it felt as the presence of God?

C: Raphael is my main angelic contact on this. His response is, "Sometimes both. When we are in the presence of God, or an angelic choir, we basically get our mission downloaded." To equate it with contemporary Earth times, he's showing me something that resembles a USB stick, but it's more sophisticated than that. It's downloaded into their consciousness what their next mission is. But sometimes when there are councils, hierarchies of Angels that meet, then there are discussions and there are teams assembled to carry out certain protocols.

R: Do these collective Angelic and supernatural beings dwell in their conversations with each other on how to help mankind... whether to help mankind, when to help mankind, or any other general categories, in other words? And something beyond mankind, too, that's the rest of the story.

C: He says that's right.

R: They may have other civilizations on their agenda...

C: They do have other aspects, that's for sure. But since we're dealing with mankind, they're going to focus on answering that part of your question. They're saying they're not really allowed to interfere with mankind to any great degree. There must be several – they're not wanting to use this word, but there's no other way to describe it – "supplicants," who are praying for the same type of assistance in order for them to be able to move in and effectively make changes in a big way. Unless there is a will of God that overrides an order saying, "Abort, abort. Let's start over again," or whatever it might be.

Primarily the whole experimentation of mankind has been to allow us to have this realization dawn on us that while we are a part of the Oneness, we are a part of Divinity made flesh; and that there is no shame in requesting help at various times. In fact, there is much more power when a collaborative effort is put forth. And part of their mission is to sometimes wait and see until it reaches critical mass level, where a lot of beings are focused on the same global decisions rather than personal ones. But personal ones, too; they say they can intervene or assist much more effectively with our request or permission.

R: I will hit this issue again later with something a lot more plausible, but right now, I asked if the Angels influence aliens in the same way that they influence humans, in a previous time. I was told that they try, but many alien civilizations are very old and have advanced capabilities of their own. This answer implies that the Angels that watch over Earth may be quite young compared to other life forms in the galaxy. So, at the risk of being impolite and offensive, I ask, how old are you guys?

C: (Chuckling) How old are the angels?

R: I know it's difficult sometimes to convey numbers so let's try this – given that theuniverse is thought to be 13.7 billion years old, and the Earth is thought to be about 4 billion years old, would you fall into the range of years associated with Earth's existence? And more narrowly, would you have been around before the Annunaki, or after?

C: They're saying that's an excellent question once again, Ray, and commend you for your curiosity. They say that their presence originated post-Annunaki, and that in fact, many alien civilizations were thought to be gods, and had something to do with populating the Earth, and other planets, too... with not only people, but animals and plant life and so forth. But they add that it's often considered blasphemous to talk about that in broad terms to most people, but that God, His or Herself, the Supreme Being, could very likely be thought of as an alien life form.

R: Wow... that's prophetic. Are they an alien life form?

C: Well, they're saying, "Where do you think the Anunnaki, and all those alien life forms came from? They did not just appear on their own."

R: I know, but I thought I just heard them say that you could think of God the Creator as an alien life form...

C: Right. As more of an original alien energy body, they're saying, rather than one that is confined to a specific physical body.

R: If that's the case, then the question is, if you were here after the Annunaki showed up, then you witnessed the engineering of mankind. Were you formerly living as humans on Earth? In other words, did you derive from humanity, or were you injected into the scene to sort of rectify the problems that arose through this engineering effort on the part of the Annunaki? Which when I read about it, it doesn't look like that was a smooth operation.

C: (Laughs) No, it was kind of an experimentation gone wild, from what I've read. Raphael is saying, "We are messengers of hope and light that, much like your earlier question about original soul creation; the Creator, Supreme Being, whatever you want to call God, realized that there needed to be this balance and counterbalance, and to give the creation of mankind hope and a voice. Simply a way to feel connected because the Annunaki and any other alien civilizations that were involved in the populating of the Earth as well as some other planets were not the best at interacting in many ways with their creations, and certainly not in compassionate ways.

For example, they very often decided to obliterate/erase those creations and start fresh, rather than giving them an opportunity to make a course correction or to improve themselves. And the Supreme Being Godhead realized, 'No! You just can't continue to create and erase. For souls to learn and grow, there needs to be this ability to have Free Will; also, not to feel alone in the universe... to have a sense of hope and a drive. Something to look forward to other than decimation and desolation.'"

R: This question is for the Archangels, and the question is, did you have to go through a lot of training in Heaven to become archangels? I don't think you just started that way, did you?

C: Michael says, "No, there were no Archangels when we first came forth. It's rather like going through military training and advancement in many ways. It's a similar progression – going through developing a number of skillsets and abilities that were not immediately within our wheelhouse." So yes, you're right – there was a lot of training, and those in the various designations of Angelic realms became apparent as they sort of earned their stripes, if you will, he says.

R: So, there must be echelons of capability above the current Archangels that did the training, and they're doing that again and again. There are Archangels graduating from advanced officer school all over the universe. Is that roughly true?

C: He says that's a good way of putting it, and some Archangels choose to evolve more into the realm of Ascended Masters, or to work more closely with Ascended Masters once they reach that higher level of angelic hierarchy rather than to stay relegated and kind of stuck. They have that option if they choose, to work more within the realm of Ascended Masters and spirit guides. But he says, "Our overall mission, no matter what our rank, is that of messenger."

Heavenly Beings: Ascended Masters

R: Are the people referred to as Ascended Masters formerly humans or other mortals who have spent their existence searching for knowledge and continue that search in Heaven? In other words, is Heaven sort of a continuation of their prior existence?

C: Gabriel responds, "Absolutely in many ways, and a lot of the members of The Brotherhood of Light (aka Ascended Masters), have never been mortal, but because it was realized long ago that to understand physical existence and to work with guiding humans, it was necessary for there to be representation of those who actually walked the Earth plane and understood many of its restrictions, many of its blessings. And so yes, it is always a continuation, and he says many of them in that category have had multiple incarnations.

Some Other Famous People

R: There has been research here in the United States that suggests that George Washington, Thomas Jefferson, and Benjamin Franklin along with other leaders were visited by and/or heavily influenced by aliens or Heavenly beings. Is that true?

C: Yes, and there were others of the Founding Fathers included in some of those meetings; but those were the main ones.

R: Is there any implication that there was special insight provided by any of these entities to any or all the writers in the composition of the United States Constitution?

C: Absolutely. And they're saying there is a lot of tongue-in-cheek verbiage in there too, talking about, and he's underlining this, "inalienable rights." He says there's a lot of double entendre that most people don't read into that, but that some of the alien influence was brought to bear in that.

Jefferson, Washington, and Franklin also, although it feels like with Franklin, even though he was obviously a great statesman in his own right, they were most interested in working with him on many of his inventions and his own writings and so forth.

But with the other two, they say, "We have observed that without certain structures being in place, it almost always leads to revolution of the people and some of this cannot be prevented." Michael adds a prime example of that was the American Civil War. There are always issues that arise when a large number of populists are involved, that often don't seem to be able to be resolved peacefully.

Another example they give is that the United States fought so hard for separation from England, the crown and that rule, that these aliens came forth just to try and do their best to share their wisdom and be sounding boards to for them as they were creating the various aspects of the Constitution.

An Alien Benefactor

R: The lady named Ambar Annati, also known as Victoria, is married to an Anunnaki man. This might imply that she is not Anunnaki. She is unlikely to be human, in view of her skills at destroying the facility at Dulce, New Mexico. So, is she some other alien race and if so, which one of those on Earth is she a member?

C: They're saying that she's kind of a hybrid. She has more of a human appearance that she can choose to display so as to pass without resistance when she is infiltrating places. But she also has a shape-shifting capability; it feels that she is part of the different strain of aliens, a hybrid combination of human with the other. They're not telling me the name of the alien race that she is a part of, but that's where she learned her cloaking or shape-shifting abilities.

R: She is reported to have been so angry at the behavior of the government agencies that helped build this Dulce facility that she didn't want to have anything to do with them and left for parts unknown. Also, we learned she had a baby from in vitro fertilization. I questioned, how she could leave her child behind? I was told her child was sent to her wherever she was.

Is she a player at the Roundtable discussions?

C: That's the sense that I get, that she will be there as a representative and as an ambassador of a galactic council... to present evidence not unlike what we see in our Senate and in the UK's Parliament; kind of tiered seating in the round of all of these different races and representatives in what is a stylized conceptual way of them each being heard and being listened to and presenting what evidence they have. So, it does feel that she is one of the players in that.

R: She seems like the kind of person you'd want to meet.

Part 17: On Seeing Spirits

Just in case we are confronted with manifested Heavenly beings!

Identifying Spirits

R: This brings me to a question of what Spirits look like relative to their former bodies, and what if a spirit never had a body? Naturally, I am curious what you Archangels would look like to someone who was formerly a human mortal, such as my father or my wife. How would you look to me as a mortal should you manifest yourself? Do you always present yourselves in the likeness of the viewer, or is there a way Angels present themselves uniquely so that they are readily recognized?

Sharon told me that she has seen beings as they take on the form of a blue energy field when they travel, but I do not know whether they are spirit or corporeal bodies that have special energy forms to facilitate travel.

I've also been told recognition of one being for another maybe something like telepathic resonance.

Can you enlighten this mortal who has seen nothing but other mortals, so far as I have recognized? It seems to me that mankind is in for some shocking visual experience including both mortal aliens and possibly immortal Heavenly beings made manifest. A little advance notice on what to expect may help smooth the way.

C: Michael's comeback to that is that the color entities are more the pure essence of spirit; others in the spirit realms can recognize each other by their frequency and vibration as well as by their color, but that would take too long for earthlings to adjust to and to understand.

Sometimes human beings do see streaks of color or colors on the floor, walls or out in nature for which there is no explanation. Sometimes when we do have visitors just checking in on us that do not want to fully manifest to us, we may catch a glimpse of a color. But by and large they tend to take on a corporeal appearance when they want to manifest. Here he cites the movie *Michael*, where John Travolta played Archangel Michael taking on human form and coming back to Earth.

Angels can essentially appear in whatever way they choose, and he's also talking about the angels that appeared to Lot and told him that they needed to leave Sodom and Gomorrah because God was going to rain down fire and brimstone on those wicked cities. Those Angels were more human in appearance so as not to overly frightened or cause problems.

Angels often can masquerade as humans, just for ease of communication and not to cause a lot of skepticism or fear. So, what we're likely to see, he says, is more of those kinds of manifestations on the Earth plane, so as to be more easily accepted. But angels can essentially appear in whatever form they want. They could also appear as animals. There are different people that believe that a soul of a pet that they have, was human or possibly is a Guardian Angel to them and he says who's to say that that's too far fetched?

Bibliography

DVD Courses

DVD Courses in Physics/Mathematics

Superstring Theory - James Gates, Jr.

Quantum Mechanics - Benjamin Schumacher

Understanding Gravity - Benjamin Schumacher

Einstein's Relativity - Richard Wolfson

The Higgs Boson & Beyond - Sean Carroll

Dark Matter, Dark Energy: The Dark Side of the Universe - Sean Carroll

Mysteries of Modern Physics: Time - Sean Carroll

Black Holes - Alex Fillipenko

Nanotechnology - Shana Kelly, Ted Sargent

Complexity - Scott Page

Chaos - Stephen Strogatz

Probability - Michael Starbird

Visual Mathematics - Michael Starbird

An Introduction to Number Theory - Edward Burger

What Einstein Got Wrong - Dan Hooper
The Physics of History - David Helfand
Understanding the Quantum World - Erica Carlson
Physics Beyond the Edge - Benjamin Schumacher
The Theory of Everything - Don Lincoln
The Great Questions of Philosophy and Physics - Steven Gimbel

DVD Courses in Philosophy and Science

Science Wars - Steven Goldman
Philosophy of Mind - Patrick Grimm
Masters of Greek Thought - Robert Bartlett
The Surveillance State - Paul Rozenzweig
Thinking About Cybersecurity - Paul Rozenzweig
Understanding the Misconceptions of Science - Don Lincoln
Experiencing Hubble - David Meyer
The Theory of Evolutio - Edward Larsen
The Philosophy of Humor - Steven Gimbel
Great Questions of Philosophy and Physics - Steven Gimbel
Mathematics, Philosophy & Real World - Judith Grabiner
An Introduction to Formal Logic - Steven Gimbel
Mysteries of the Microscopic World - Bruce Fleury
The Science of Self - Lee M. Silver
Human Perception - Peter M. Vishton
Game Theory - Scott Stevens
The Aging Brain - Thad Polk
Human Body: How We Fail, How We Heal - Anthony Goodman
The Spiritual Brain - Andrew Newberg
Passions: Philosophy, Intelligence of Emotions - Robert Solomon

BOOKS

Physics
The Physics of Immortality - Frank Tippler

The Singularity is Near - Ray Kurzweil
*Hyperspace*Michio Kaku *Physics of the Impossible* - Michio Kaku
Parallel Worlds - Michio Kaku
Physics of the Future - Michio Kaku
The Physics of God - Joseph Selbie
Brief Answers to Big Questions - Stephen Hawking

Physics, Ethics, Politics
The Philosophy of Aristotle - Barbara Jancar
Ten Philosophical Mistakes - Mortimer J. Adler
Space from Zeno to Einstein - Nick Huggett
Introduction to Objectivist Epistemology - Ayn Rand
The Virtue of Selfishness - Ayn Rand
For The New Intellectual - Ayn Rand
The New Left: The Anti-Industrial Revolution - Ayn Rand
The Romantic Manifesto - Ayn Rand
Capitalism: The Unknown Ideal - Ayn Rand
The True Believer - Eric Hoffer
The Passionate State Of Mind - Eric Hoffer
The Temper of Our Time - Eric Hoffer
The Ordeal of Change - Eric Hoffer
God Games - Neil Freer
Animal Farm - George Orwell
1984 - George Orwell
Brave New World - Aldous Huxley
The War Prayer - Mark Twain

Biology
The Tangled Tree - David Quammen
The Mosquito: A Human History - Timothy Winegard

Philosophical/Moral Fiction
The Fountainhead - Ayn Rand
Atlas Shrugged - Ayn Rand

Anthem - Ayn Rand
We The Living - Ayn Rand

Biblical
King James Version - Various
New American, New English - Various
Missing Books of the Bible - Unknown
The Book of Mormon - Joseph Smith
LDS Doctrines and Covenants - Joseph Smith
The Missing Books of the Bible Vols. I & II - Unknown

Islam
The Sword of the Prophet - Serge Trifkovik

Pre-History (mostly pre-4000 B.C.)
The Supergods - Maurice Cottrell
Deep Truths - Gregg Braden
The Book of Enoch the Prophet - R.H. Charles
*Myths from Mesopotamia*Stephanie Dalley
The Epic of Gilgamesh - Betty Radice
History is Wrong - Erich von Däniken
Pathways to the Gods (The Stones of Kiribati) - Erich von Däniken
Odyssey of the Gods - Erich von Däniken
The Destruction of Atlantis - Frank Joseph
Survivors of Atlantis - Frank Joseph
The Gods of Eden - William Bramley
The 12th Planet - Zechariah Sitchin
The Lost Realms - Zechariah Sitchin
When Time Began - Zechariah Sitchin
The Stairway to Heaven - Zechariah Sitchin
The Wars of Gods and Men - Zechariah Sitchin
The Cosmic Code - Zechariah Sitchin
Divine Encounters - Zechariah Sitchin
Of Heaven and Earth - Zechariah Sitchin

The Lost Book of Enki - Zechariah Sitchin
The Earth Chronicles Expeditions - Zechariah Sitchin
Journey to the Mythical Past - Zechariah Sitchin
The End of Days - Zechariah Sitchin
The Earth Chronicles Handbook - Zechariah Sitchin
The Anunnaki Encyclopedia Vol. I - Maximillien De Lafayette
The Anunnaki Encyclopedia Vol. II - Maximillien De Lafayette
DNA of the Gods - Chris Hardy

Archeology, Exploration, Unorthodox Science

Lost Star - Walter Crittendon
Beneath The Pyramids - Andrew Collins
Gobekli Tepe: Genesis of The Gods - Andrew Collins, Shaun Grindell
Lost Knowledge of the Ancients - Graham Hancock
Fingerprints of the Gods - Graham Hancock
Underworld - Graham Hancock

Modern Evidence of Aliens

The Monuments of Mars - Richard Hoagland
Dark Mission - Hoagland and Bara
Sight Unseen - Hopkins and Rainey
Ancient Aliens TV Series - The History Channel

Paranormal Capabilities

The Field - Lynne McTaggart
Mutant Message Down Under - Marlo Morgan
The Mysterious Stranger - Mark Twain
A Christmas Carol - Charles Dickens
The Once and Future King - T.H. White
The Collected Stories of Ambrose Bierce - Ambrose Bierce

Near Death Experiences

The Application of Impossible Things - Natalie Sudman

Ninety Minutes in Heaven - Don Piper
On Death and Dying - Elisabeth Kübler-Ross
On Life After Death - Elisabeth Kübler-Ross

Reincarnation, Past Lives
Journey of Souls - Michael Newton
Destiny of Souls - Michael Newton
Many Lives, Many Masters - Brian Weiss

Mediums and Talking to Those In 9 Dimensions
Johnny Angel is My Brother: A Psychic Medium's Journey - Cheryl E. Booth
Survival of the Soul - Lisa Williams
The Law of Attraction - Esther and Jerry Hicks
Between Death and Life - Dolores Cannon
The Custodians - Dolores Cannon
Jesus and the Essenes - Dolores Cannon
There is a River - Thomas Sugrue
(Biography of Edgar Cayce, "The Sleeping Prophet")

Recommended Films & Series About Metaphysics, The Afterlife, Aliens, A.I., Time Travel, Etc.

NOTE: *As with the books and courses mentioned above, this is by no means a totally comprehensive list, but rather some films the authors have found particularly enjoyable and good food for thought. Enjoy!*

What Dreams May Come
Somewhere in Time
Ghost
Defending Your Life
What the Bleep Do We Know
It's a Wonderful Life
Dead Again
Jesus Christ Superstar
Superman (1978)
The Man Who Fell to Earth
Bicentennial Man
Starman
A.I.
Star Wars: A New Hope (original film)
Altered States

Hereafter

The Good Place (TV series available on Netflix at the time of this book's publication)

Quantum Leap (TV series from the 1980s and early '90s)

The Time Traveler's Wife

Conversations With God

The Five People You Meet in Heaven

The Way of the Peaceful Warrior

Waking Life

Harry Potter and the Prisoner of Azkaban

The Fountain

The Tree of Life

Bruce Almighty

2001: A Space Odyssey

The Sixth Sense

Life of Brian

The Last Temptation of Christ

The Da Vinci Code

Angels and Demons

E.T.

Close Encounters of the Third Kind

Contact

Epilogue

Some questions may arise in the minds of some that need further clarification and we are dedicated to seeking that clarification in future conversations with Heavenly sources. Things on Earth have obviously changed in a huge way due to the global impact of COVID-19.

We believe that as the human race continues to experience more change, it is wise to be an informed population, but not a fearful one. The Creator is mindful of our needs and within the context of His purpose, acts accordingly. Our free will can be considered a tipping point in the velocity of our soul growth.

Be sure to claim your FREE Bonus Audios (keep reading). And if you have questions for Ray or Cheryl, please feel free to direct them to the following email address:

Cosmictalkshow@gmail.com

Bonuses!
And...Before You Go

We are so grateful that you have taken this cosmic/celestial journey with us in our book. We thank you from the bottom of our hearts and wish you all the very best. Stay safe and healthy in these ever-changing times in which we all are living.

Ray and Cheryl would like to ask you a favor: If you enjoyed the book, please take just a few minutes to write a quick review on our Amazon page. Just go to Amazon and search *Cosmic Talk Show* under books, and it will pop up.

As an additional Thank You for buying the book, if you'd like to receive any or all of Cheryl's audios FREE, you may request them by writing to

Cosmictalkshow@gmail.com

The audios are:

- *Be Your Own Medium* (contains tips for strengthening your direct communication with loved ones in Spirit)
- *Livin' La Vida Stressless* (A light relaxing form of hypnosis to help relieve stress)
- *Ancient Chakra Toning Secrets* (A great way to balance and regroup, feel grounded and centered)

When you make your request by email, just list which audios you'd like to receive, and a link will be sent to you from Dropbox.com

Thank You and Bless You!

Cheryl and Ray